Nothing Can Separate Us

Nothing Can Separate Us

C. W. Bess

BROADMAN PRESS
Nashville, Tennessee

© Copyright 1986 • Broadman Press
All Rights Reserved
4222-63
ISBN: 0-8054-2263-3
Dewey Decimal Classification: 227.1
Subject Headings: BIBLE N. T. ROMANS 8:35-39 — SERMONS
Library of Congress Catalog Number: 8668-39
Printed in the United States of America

Unless otherwise stated, all Scripture quotations are from the Revised Standard Version of the Bible, copyrighted 1946, 1952, © 1971, 1973.

Scripture quotations marked KJV are from the King James Version of the Bible.

Scripture quotations marked Phillips are reprinted with permission of Macmillan Publishing Co., Inc. from J. B. Phillips: *The New Testament in Modern English,* Revised Edition. © J. B. Phillips 1958, 1960, 1972.

Library of Congress Cataloging-in-Publication Data

Bess, C. W., 1942-
  Nothing can separate us.

  1. Bible. N.T. Romans VIII, 35-39—Criticism, interpretation, etc. 2. Christian life—1960-
I. Title.
BS2665.2.B47 1986   227'.106   86-6839
ISBN 0-8054-2263-3

To the members of
Central Baptist Church
in Jacksonville, Texas

"I thank my God in all my remembrance of you, always in every prayer of mine for you all making my prayer with joy, thankful for your partnership in the gospel from the first day until now" (Phil. 1: 3-5).

Acknowledgments

No matter how macho we men try to act, we still depend upon those special ladies in our lives who make us look good. For this writer it begins at home where Mary, my mate in both marriage and ministry, encourages me in writing. These projects require discipline, late hours of study, and energy that could be used in being a better husband. All pastors should be so blessed to have a Mary Bess.

Gina Ginsel never tires of typing my articles for various publications. As pastor's secretary, she transforms dictated tapes via a word processor into readable manuscripts. Just as amazing is how she deciphers my sloppy scrawl when I occasionally revert to yellow legal pads. Gina is ever efficient and always cheerful.

Anne Hendry, my local proofreader and seeker of elusive errors, remains a forever friend through many manuscripts. She is a creative writer herself, a gracious grammarian, and adviser in the written word.

Anne Hall joined the team by reading the final draft and making valuable suggestions. As a schoolteacher, Anne can spot a vague pronoun or a missing antecedent a mile away!

Grateful appreciation is due the *Jacksonville Daily Progress* in whose pages much of this material was first published as my regular column "The Central Idea." Some ideas appeared in *The*

Pulpit Digest as "Homeletic Bias," another by-line of several years. Yet other thoughts were printed in *Proclaim* magazine.

C. W. Bess
Jacksonville, Texas

Contents

Acknowledgments vii
Introduction 11
Part One: Nothing Can Separate Us—Not Even 17
   Tribulation 18
   Distress 20
   Persecution 24
   Famine 26
   Nakedness 30
   Peril 33
   Sword 36
Part Two: No, Nothing Can Separate Us—Not Even 41
   Death 42
   Life 47
   Angels 50
   Principalities 53
   Things Present 54
   Things to Come 57
   Powers 60
   Height 63
   Depth 66
Part Three: Nor Anything Else in All Creation 69
   Survival Kit 70
   Secrets 71
   Rewards 73
   Disease Defeated 75
   Stewardship 77
   The Greater Plan 78
   The Last Word 80
   Determination 82

Affliction	83
Faith and Works	85
Self-Interest	86
A Missouri Miracle	88
Our Advocate	90
Perfect Sight	92
Break a Leg	94
The Choice	95
Change	97
Nothing New?	99
Perseverance	100
Payday Someday	102
Escape	103
Determined	105
Wisdom	107
Failure	109
The Past Is Past	111
Born Loser	114
Moderation	115
Value	117
Follow-up	119
Good News	120
Wacky Ways	121
Submission	122
A Shocking Experience	123
Out of This World	125
Renewal	126
Pobody's Nerfect	127
Together	128
Hope	130
Surrender	132
Duty	133
Index of Scripture Texts	135
Index of Names	141

Introduction

Ancient Romans would feel at home in modern America where positive people thrive on competition. We are energetic and interested in action. Like the Romans, we value freedom of expression, stable institutions, and a legal system tolerant of constant litigation.

This last trait may be one of our most glaring weaknesses. Our civil courts today are bogged down with lawsuits that can best be described as frivolous. It is not unusual for restaurant customers to sue for damages when they find a bug in the salad. They cite "emotional distress."

A married couple from Towson, Maryland, tried to sue owners of the Baltimore Colts who moved that team to Indianapolis. They contended that as loyal fans they had suffered irreparable emotional harm upon learning the bad news. Along with their demands for financial reparations, they insisted a federal judge force the team owners to cancel their moving plans and remain in Baltimore!

That happened in the civil court system, but our criminal law system allows similar nonsense. Not long ago an appeals court ordered one warden to provide a personal computer to a Great Falls, Montana, convict. It seems that the prisoner had filed so many different appeals, only a computer could keep track of his legal situation. To safeguard the prisoner's rights, therefore, the constitution guaranteed a computer to that inmate.

Sometimes the logic of legal appeals soars to a questionable level. After years of innovative appeals to avoid a Supreme-Court-approved execution of a condemned murderer, his lawyers succeeded in yet another final reprieve based upon ridiculous logic. They argued that the lethal drug to be injected into convicted murderer Ronald C. O'Bryan was unsafe! It had yet to be approved by the Federal Drug Administration and was, thus, illegal.

The frequent use of legal terminology by New Testament writers indicates a similar preoccupation with laws and courts throughout the Roman empire. With the glaring exceptions of Pilate's capitulation to a Jewish mob and the stoning of Stephen, Roman law generally guarded the rights of early Christians. Converts were free to worship as they desired.

Spectacular success of the growing movement, however, later provoked the inevitable, negative reactions. Paul saw Christians being challenged by the same Roman law which earlier had protected them. Perhaps he envisioned the crowded coliseum scenes where condemned Christians would soon be thrown to the lions.

Even in the best of times, life is a struggle. Christians throughout the ages and even now are confronted by persecution and prison. With evil forces arrayed against us, we face overwhelming odds against survival. To the casual observer we appear to be doomed. Shall we quietly give up and be conquered?

Never! Defeat is not to be our fate. Look again. We may be in a worldly minority, but we are never left alone. "If God is for us, who is against us? He who did not spare his own Son but gave him up for us all, will he not also give us all things with him?" (Rom. 8:31-32).

Few passages of Scripture communicate so clearly to Americans as chapter 8 of Romans. While several great doctrines are briefly touched, the discussion never mires down in ponderous depth. These are mountain peaks of inspiration equally exciting to new converts and seasoned scholars. The action moves at a rapid pace in an approach which presents a positive plus for believers. We are winners and more than conquerors.

These are timeless ideas expressed to the church located in the empire's capital city. They cut easily across cultural lines to strike a responsive chord in our hearts today.

This eighth chapter of Romans includes many legal analogies in a series of questions raised and firmly answered.

> Who shall bring any charge against God's elect? It is God who justifies; who is to condemn? Is it Christ Jesus, who died, yes who was raised from the dead, who is at the right hand of God, who indeed intercedes for us? (Rom. 8:33-34).

At this point in his ministry, Paul had already felt the sting of unjust charges. He had been illegally stoned by a mob which left him for dead outside Lystra. He had suffered other setbacks and would become the target of more false charges. Soon he would defend himself before a succession of officials in a legal appeal carried all the way to Rome. In that capital the first readers of this letter would minister to his daily needs until his execution.

Paul never doubted that with Jesus ready to intercede for us, the final decision will be in our favor. We are ultimate winners, not losers, destined to be "more than conquerors." Thus Paul moved toward the positive conclusion of Romans 8 confronting real and imagined fears of Christians under challenge.

What is your darkest fear? Or do you have a personal phobia which is your worst imagined fate? Some are afraid of heights while others worry about closed places or darkness. People fear germs, crowds, or even birds and bees.

The greatest fear of all humanity, however, is being cut off, separated, or left alone. We feel safer in a crowd. Hitler's grim executioners made efficient use of the human fear of being left behind. During World War II six million Jews were herded like sheep to an obvious slaughter. Why did they not resist even within the shadow of gas chambers and human ovens? European Jews, always the minority, huddled together for security. Hitler's henchmen recognized that trait and always kept the condemned tightly packed together. Very few prisoners ever bolted from the mutual comfort or danger of the group.

No one wants to be left behind by accident. To be purposely pushed aside or cut off is even worse. Primitive societies and modern cults practice an ultimate form of discipline at this point. It is a devastating form of social isolation sometimes called *shunning*.

The unfortunate person being punished is treated as a dead person. Neither family nor friends are permitted to speak to the outcast or even acknowledge his presence. Some orthodox Jews even impose this treatment upon a child who marries outside the faith.

What a cruel treatment! Solitary confinement or total rejection is a fate feared worse than death. Even in a prison filled with social misfits and violent inmates, no prisoner desires to be left alone for very long.

To be forsaken or forgotten by God is probably the ultimate fear of all people. When Jesus took the sins of everyone in the world on Himself and hung on the cross suspended between heaven and earth, the physical pain of crucifixion paled before the spiritual agony of feeling abandoned by the Almighty. "My God, my God, why hast thou forsaken me?" (Matt. 27:47).

With these thoughts in mind, Paul asked: "Who shall separate us from the love of Christ?" (Rom. 8:35). There follows a list of human fears picked, not at random, but from bitter, personal experience. Those were Paul's own fears. How common and similar to ours.

The list is representative but not all inclusive. Some scholars endlessly analyze the structure of his list or wonder about conspicuous omissions. Why did he not include Satan as the very first of these fears? Disease, illness, and personal injuries are also excluded.

Rather than speculate on Paul's silence, we will begin with what he said. We follow his own outline which appears in three sections or groups of fears. Verse 35 presents the first group of seven challenges beginning with tribulation. Verses 38-39 provide the second section with a final division suggested by Paul's sweeping phrase, "nor anything else in all creation." None of these negative forces or challenges can succeed in separating us from the love of Christ.

If only we could "comprehend with all the saints what is the breath and length and height and depth, and to know the love of Christ which surpasses knowledge, that you may be filled with all the fulness of God" (Eph. 3:18-19).

This is a favorite theme often expressed in Pauline theology. The solution to our fears is found in a faith based upon the unlimited love of Jesus. Our own strength is not the key. We prevail through God's love in Christ Jesus.

No one can successfully bring false charges against God's elect. Our defense is no haphazard matter. The outcome is far better than a hung jury or a deadlocked score. We are winners and conquerors. In all these things we are *more than conquerors.*

Part One: Nothing Can Separate Us— Not Even

**Tribulation
Distress
Persecution
Famine
Nakedness
Peril
Sword**

Tribulation

Some years ago a sultry-voiced beauty challenged male television viewers: "Are you looking for trouble? Then you've found it. A little Trouble in the morning and you've got Trouble all day long. Trouble After-shave Lotion!"

This clever commercial attracted a lot of attention on the screen but little action in the marketplace. The new product did not sell well. It was probably because most of us are not really looking for trouble of any kind. But trouble comes looking for us in life. It comes in many forms and a variety of names—trial, burden, anguish, and affliction being some of the terms translated in Scripture to describe the Greek word *thlipsis.*

Yet the strongest and most accurate translation remains *tribulation,* an English term derived from the Latin *tribulum.* This was a threshing sledge or platform with sharp metal points. Corn and other grains were shelled by the rough, rubbing action. Imagine human flesh rubbed against a *tribulum!* That was tribulation.

Jesus warned of a great tribulation to come "such as has not been from the beginning of the world." He described dark days when "the sun will be darkened, and the moon will not give its light, and the stars will fall from heaven, and the powers of the heavens will be shaken" (Matt. 24:21, 29).

That was the "great tribulation," a fright-filled end to an era described also in The Revelation to John. Perhaps because of that apocalyptic association, this term sounds overly dramatic in describing daily life.

Yet the word is frequently used in the New Testament, and a majority of those occasions indicate ordinary struggles instead of a world-ending catastrophe. Paul considered tribulation to be such a daily challenge that he listed it first among things which should not separate us from the love of Christ. In his parting words of comfort to the disciples in Lystra, Iconium, and Antioch, Paul explained "that through many tribulations we must enter the kingdom of God" (Acts 14:22).

Tribulation is often mentioned in company with other negative ideas such as persecution, distress, and poverty. But the experience need not always be negative. Jesus spoke of worldly tribulations as an opportunity to be of good cheer. "In the world you have tribulation, but be of good cheer, I have overcome the world" (John 16:33).

Paul echoed our Lord's sentiments in Romans 5:3-5.

> More than that we rejoice in our sufferings ["tribulations," KJV] knowing that suffering produces endurance, and endurance produces character, and character produces hope and hope does not disappoint us, because God's love has been poured into our hearts through the Holy Spirit which has been given to us.

What a challenging thought! Rather than complain about our tribulations, we can thank God for them in expectation and confidence of things better. "We know that in everything God works for good with those who love him, who are called according to his purpose" (Rom. 8:28).

When confronted with any problem, our immediate goal is to seek God's purpose. Something good will surely come from anything bad, if we let God work with us.

In 1882 a bright little girl, nineteen months of age, contracted a high fever which left her both blind and deaf. Helen Keller would never hear the lovely sound of birds singing in the forest. She would never see the beautiful sight of flowers blooming in a garden.

How would you respond to such a dismal and discouraging future? Helen retreated into her own shadow of darkness and isolation. Her only expressions toward others were outbursts of rage and anger. She refused to cooperate in any way with life.

But then God sent Ann Sullivan to help that pitiful problem child. Miss Annie understood, for she herself had grown up blind until an operation gave her sight at age sixteen. Slowly the new teacher broke into Helen's life, offering hope while demanding discipline. After long years of agonizing and patient work, Helen learned to read, talk, write, and demonstrate that with God all things are possible. They became a famous team, bringing encouragement to handicapped people all over the world.

So inspiring was Helen Keller's life that she regularly received invitations from the White House. Miss Keller personally visited every American President from her teenage years until 1968 when she died at age eighty-eight. No other person in American history comes close to duplicating that feat.

Hear her testimony. Miss Keller was fond of saying in public to her teacher: "Miss Annie, I thank God every day of my life for sending you to me."

About her affliction, Miss Keller explained: "The marvelous richness of human experience would lose something of rewarding joy if there were no limitations to overcome."

Did you catch that? She viewed her own trouble or tribulation as "limitations to overcome" and "something of rewarding joy." With God's help she learned that in a world of many tribulations, one can still "be of good cheer" (John 16:33). She knew how to rejoice in all things.

Distress

You are exhausted while trudging alone toward home. A stranger ahead leans against a brick wall and casually reads a newspaper, yet he does not seem relaxed or interested in his reading. You sense something is wrong. The man may be a mugger. Your heart beats faster as adrenaline surges through your system. Fright signals your muscles to go on alert, preparing you for fight or flight. You feel an intense distress before realizing the stranger has turned and gone.

On another occasion you drop by your physician's office for a routine exam. Doctors are trained to interpret physical signs of distress revealed by your body which may be related to injury, disease, or poor nutrition. Modern physicians also watch for emotional overload caused by the grinding pressure of daily life. They describe it simply as stress.

European explorers of Africa stumbled upon a strange but effective test for untruth based upon this idea of observable stress. Primitive tribesmen practiced a test of the white-hot spear, a procedure which invariably worked.

Following any serious crime, all villagers were questioned by the witch doctor. If no one confessed, then every suspect lined up to witness a spear point heated until it glowed white hot.

The test was simple. Every suspect stuck out his tongue to be touched by the hot metal. They believed that a truthful tongue would not be harmed. Only a tongue which tells untruth would be burned.

You know what usually happened. The guilty person would bolt into the bushes as the spear approached. Case solved!

But what if no one ran? This truth test still worked. Down the line the hot spear moved, touching tongues without harm until one person screamed in pain. He was the guilty one.

Superstition? Not at all. This procedure used the same scientific principle as snuffing out a candle flame between thumb and forefinger. As every parlor magician knows, you must first lick your finger and thumb before quickly squeezing the flame. For that brief second your skin is protected by the moisture.

Under normal conditions the tongue is moist enough to prevent a quick burn from a candle flame or hot metal. The innocent suspects who waited in line for the hot spear point may not have understood why this test worked, but they trusted the results and relaxed. No problem. But the guilty person under intense stress found it impossible to relax. His body muscles tensed. His mouth became dry. Soon he was betrayed by his own tongue which burned for lack of protective moisture.

The physical body reveals the secrets of guilt through signs of stress. That was the basic principle behind the white-hot spear. Today it supposedly works with modern polygraph instruments, better known as lie detectors. They measure blood pressure, heart rate, perspiration, and other physical signs of stress associated with a guilty conscience.

The apostle Paul didn't worry about past sins causing him distress. He confessed them and found release from God. Still he bore in his body many scars from exhaustion, disease, and physical abuse by enemies of the cross. He knew firsthand the pain of feeling cut off and the doubts that God had deserted him. Thus, he included distress as second in a list of problems which might separate us from God.

How interesting that some people bloom best under stress. They push themselves, try harder, and refuse to take defeat lying down. Such was a sickly child born in 1858 and destined for greatness. But he had much to overcome.

Even his name sounded soft and sissy. Theodore was the sickly child other boys liked to push around. But once they pushed him too far. After being thrashed by a neighborhood bully, the child made a determined vow to get tough. No more running away. Back out into the playground he went, ready to face the distress of past defeat.

No, he did not become a Charles Atlas or modern-day Samson. In fact, he continued to wear spectacles the rest of his life. But Teddy Roosevelt became a man's man excelling in sports like boxing and big-game hunting. His vocations varied from cowpoke to cavalry officer.

Colonel Roosevelt became a hero in the Spanish-American War. His brave charge up San Juan Hill inspired a major victory and propelled him into the White House where he took a bullet in the chest from a would-be assassin. After the man was subdued, Roosevelt refused medical attention until after he finished his speech!

Yes, T. R. Roosevelt was some tough cookie. And it all began from a beating at the hands of a neighborhood bully. He made the best out of his brokenness. Refusing to wallow in bitterness or self-pity, Roosevelt took something bad and made something better.

Call it dividends from defeat—profit from pitfalls. It's our choice made possible by a God who urges us to victory over life's distressing defeats.

Paul would have understood Roosevelt's physical distress. He explained to the Corinthians how God had humbled him with "a thorn in the flesh," possibly some disease which caused constant discomfort and pain. Three times he sought the Lord to remove it before God's answer finally came. "My grace is sufficient for you, for my power is made perfect in weakness" (2 Cor. 12:9).

The cause of distress was not removed as requested. Instead, Paul learned to lean more on God's grace, which is sufficient for every need. Not relief from pain, but reliance upon God. God's power is made complete in our weakness.

Rather than causing separation, distress can actually help draw us closer to the Lord. Life is stressful. These daily tensions stretch our horizons and strengthen us. We must learn to live with distress accompanied by God's daily comfort. He helps us cope.

"Therefore, I take pleasure in infirmities, in reproaches, in necessities, in persecutions, in distresses for Christ's sake; for when I am weak, then I am strong" (2 Cor. 12:10, KJV).

Persecution

The stooped President arrived in a rumpled suit and a dusty top hat. He had slept fitfully the night before because Americans were dying in record numbers. Victory was uncertain as people gathered at this battlefield to dedicate a national cemetery where thousands had fallen.

Most officials did not expect the President to appear. A prominent speaker (now forgotten by many) was assigned the major speech, with the President being given only a token part in the program as an afterthought.

After speaking briefly with the aid of notes jotted on an envelope, the President sat down. Applause was noticeably subdued.

Major newspapers responded with hostile reviews. The *Patriot and Union* concluded: "We pass over the silly remarks of the president . . . willing that the veil of oblivion shall be dropped over them that they shall no more be respected or thought of."

The *Chicago Times* editorialized: "The cheek of every American must tingle with shame as he reads the silly, flat, and dishwatery utterances of the man who has to be pointed out to intelligent foreigners as the President of the United States."

Just who was this presidential "failure"? Abraham Lincoln had just delivered the best-remembered speech in American history—The Gettysburg Address!

Lincoln could have just as well stayed home and avoided the personal pain of a public persecution. But he did not allow his critics that satisfaction. He realized they would find fault whatever his course of action, so he did as he felt right.

Later generations saw what contemporaries of that beleaguered

President missed. The long look of history helps us appreciate the struggles of this wartime leader and understand better his genuine character. Again and again he rose above putdowns and persecutions.

Scholars who have read his letters and studied his life now admire his quiet strength so clearly drawn from a deep faith in God. The Bible which he had studied permeated his soul and was even reflected in his writing style. He found courage to stay on course doing what he sensed was best to keep America together.

Of course, the opposition or personal criticism leveled against us does not necessarily mean the same as persecution. Sometimes we bring these things on ourselves as did the two thieves dying on either side of Jesus. We are often too quick to perceive ourselves as being persecuted and too slow to admit our own faults. In some bitter confrontations neither side can claim the high ground.

A few Christians are so combative and aggressive by nature that they are always spoiling for a fight. They are happiest when involved in conflict. When the inevitable counterattack comes against them, they wrap themselves in the robes of self-righteousness and scream about persecution. They seem to have a martyr's complex which invites persecution. Unfortunately, they prefer doing battle with other Christians over finer points of doctrine.

There is a substantial difference between deserved punishment and genuine persecution. It depends upon who is being attacked—people or God. We ought not take persecution as personally against us but rather on behalf of our Lord. "For it is for thy sake that I have borne reproach" (Ps. 69:7).

But even the genuine, godly persecution which Jesus promised us can become a heavy load to bear. According to legend, a weary Christian, burdened by a cross made heavy by persecution, stumbled into a cross maker's shop. He did not argue about bearing his own cross, but he considered his load unfair. The persecution he suffered made his cross unbearable.

"Very well," the kind carpenter said. "You may take your pick of any of may crosses used by the saints through the ages. Choose the one easiest to carry."

The man approached the stack of crosses, trying them all for size and comfort. Each seemed heavier than the last to his shoulders until he came to one which was definitely lighter than the others. He held it awhile and then concluded: "I can carry this one easily. May I take it?"

"Yes, certainly you may. But that is the same one you brought in with you," the cross maker replied. "Perhaps the persecution you perceived to suffer will no longer seem so hard to bear when compared to that burden carried by other Christians."

> Blessed are you when men revile you and persecute you and utter all kinds of evil against you for my account. Rejoice and be glad, for your reward is great in heaven, for so men persecuted the prophets who were before you (Matt. 5:11-12).

Famine

For years Malthusian doomsayers had pointed to some undeniable and unsettling facts. The total number of people in Third World nations continued to increase in a geometric progression vividly described as a "population explosion." Where would these impoverished nations find food to feed these multiplied millions? With all available farm land in use (and much of it already exhausted or in the process of severe erosion), starvation seemed certain with the next inevitable drought. A decade of famine was predicted for the 1970s.

"The Green Revolution" averted that disaster with dramatic innovations in the fields of genetics and botany. Just in the nick of time, researchers developed new hybrids of rice and other grains which yielded in bountiful crops. Within two brief years most grain-importing nations accumulated huge surpluses and became exporters of food. World food prices tumbled. Suddenly all the poor nations could afford rice again.

In the 1980s a credit crunch hovers over the world as a dark cloud. High interest rates amid a global recession threatens the less-developed nations with bankruptcy. They can't raise enough money for interest expense, let alone pay back their debts owed to large American banks. Those bad loans could lead to bank failures in America. A domino effect might then send shock waves through the American economy, causing recession or even depression. If depression comes, famine will surely follow.

The genetic botanists are still busy in their laboratories, but they can't promise another Green Revolution. To the contrary, they worry aloud about our increased reliance on a few super grains. Will this approach eventually contribute to a crop failure of unparalleled proportions? Many of today's standardized and hybridized crops are too genetically similar. A blight which kills one plant can kill millions. A new fungus wiped out 15 percent of the U.S. corn crop in 1970. The next blight could destroy all the world's corn or rice.

Where will researchers find older varieties which might provide a pool of genes which might be plague resistant? Because farmers have switched to the hybrid seeds, many plant species have completely disappeared. About seven-thousand varieties of apples, for example, have disappeared since the turn of this century.

Will the extra time given to us by science only delay the inevitable and increase the total suffering? Now we have millions more mouths to feed. The "baby bomb" may be more deadly than any enemy missile.

Famine is not a casual subject to be studied only in ancient history. It is more than an abstract fear for the distant future. Even now millions are hungry as famine continues to plague many parts of the world.

Jesus warned of famine to come in the last days. It is one of the signs of His coming and the close of the age. (Matt. 24:3-7) Many biblical prophecies warn of this certain danger. John's Revelation described the four horsemen traditionally interpreted as war, famine, pestilence, and death (Rev. 6).

The thought of starving infants is depressing. We feel so helpless seeing the magazine pictures or television stories of innocent children doomed by malnutrition. Like war and rumors of war, we know the problem cannot be completely solved.

Yet, we can do something. Like the four lepers during the Syrian siege of Samaria, we Americans eat and drink from abundance while others starve. They occupied themselves with their sudden riches, securing silver, gold, and other treasures. Still there was more than they would ever use. Finally the four men came to their senses and recognized a responsibility to share the good news of freedom and abundance.

"We are not doing right. This day is a day of good news; if we are silent and wait until the morning light, punishment will overtake us; now therefore come let us go and tell the king's household" (2 Kings 7:9).

Telling the good news about freedom and salvation is a missionary task for all. My denomination supports a large, spiritual army of over two-thousand foreign missionaries, plus many more in home missions. We share good news about Jesus which can guarantee a heavenly destiny. But we also have resources for providing food which can meet some of today's urgent need in the wake of worldwide famine.

Yes, you and I can help the starving. Any local church can channel personal gifts to organizations already ministering in crisis areas. Those who work in foreign missions consider food distribution an urgent priority. Missionaries on foreign fields are already involved in this key ministry of feeding hungry people.

Probably the most effective of these projects look beyond the temporary crisis to develop more effective solutions where local farmers produce more food. Our strategy reflects an old saying: "Give a person a fish and he will eat for a day. Teach him to fish, and he will eat for a lifetime."

In America we have the world's greatest pool of agricultural talent and basic farm knowledge. We have veterinarians and other experts in breeding and raising livestock. Our government continues to send Peace Corps workers in this critical area of self-help. But is this not a valid ministry for missionaries, too? Many retired farmers and plant specialists are needed to share their abilities with countless villages where new ideas can literally make the difference in life or death.

Sometimes these lay missionaries bring new breeding stock like rabbits or goats. Or they introduce new grains which thrive on land depleted by overemphasis of a previous crop. Irrigation, crop rotation, and a host of basic ideas can help in backward areas to provide homegrown food or create food-related industries.

This longer-range response to famine conditions answers growing criticism that our temporary programs only delay the ultimate day of worldwide starvation. It also recognizes the practical problems in delivering American surpluses to starving bodies. Much grain is lost to rodents and spoilage while en route. Bureaucratic delays and rampant corruption in recipient nations are obstacles out of our control. The free food may arrive in the intended country but wind up on the black market at exorbitant prices. In effect, our good intentions simply finance more corruption for a greedy few in power. But since when does difficulty in trying to do good allow us a justifiable excuse for doing nothing?

But the best thing we can do is not to lose hope. How easy to become discouraged—or worse, cynical. We need Paul's optimism and assurance. Satan may rejoice in so much human suffering, but God can grant victory to those who call upon Him. Anyone who believes in Jesus has hope. Although some believers are separated from the physical strength of food, they can never be separated from the love of God in Christ Jesus.

"So we do not lose heart. Though our outer nature is wasting away, our inner nature is being renewed every day" (2 Cor. 4:16).

Nakedness

An amusing fable tells how some cunning con men once convinced a king to wear royal robes that didn't really exist. He was at first hesitant, of course. Yet he did not want to admit that his eyes could not see what was so obvious to these magical tailors. Once the monarch pretended to believe in the invisible garments, everyone else in the kingdom fell into line. The ploy was exposed only by the honesty of a child who uttered the unthinkable: "The king has no clothes!"

That king was surely not Augustus III of Poland who feared nakedness but loved clothing. Before he died in 1764, his closet overflowed into two huge warehouses. His wardrobe included thousands of tailored suits coordinated with a different watch, snuffbox, cane, sword, and wig designed for each outfit.

Long ago a father gave his favored son a coat of many colors. Such obvious partiality didn't set well with the older brothers, especially when the best-dressed youth boasted about how all his family members would someday bow down to him.

That was indeed God's plan for Joseph, but the high fashion was not necessarily included. God first allowed him to be humiliated and humbled by those brothers he wanted to rule. They stripped him of his haughty coat and sold the naked youth into Egyptian slavery. Joseph would soon learn to wear the drab garments of a house servant and the coarse cloth of a prison inmate.

Between those two styles of dress, Joseph was once again caught naked. But this second time his virtue emerged rather than his vanity. His master's wife was determined to seduce the handsome youth who refused to weaken. He had learned to trust God. One day she caught him alone. In his struggle to flee, she held onto his robe, and he fled naked. That is how Joseph wound up in prison before his promotion as Pharaoh's all-powerful deputy. Nakedness, considered one of the ultimate humiliations of the ancient world, was twice used by God in Joseph's preparation for greatness.

Psychologists remind us that because we enter this world naked at birth, the condition is associated with helplessness and a lack of power. A nightmare common to many people is being caught naked in public or wearing only underwear. More than an embarrassing thought, it is sometimes a real fear.

Perhaps the fear is also related to our lack of candor or honesty. We dress for success. Nice clothing can impress people and project a better image for us in public. In a way, our clothes become a cover-up for insecurities and other fears. We don't want to be emotionally naked. God created Adam and Eve with neither sin nor clothing. "And the man and his wife were both naked, and were not ashamed" (Gen. 2:25). But not for long. They both sinned. The first obvious result of their disobedience soon became apparent. "Then the eyes of both were opened, and they knew that they were naked; and they sewed fig leaves together and made themselves aprons" (Gen. 3:7).

Next the fully clothed couple heard the sound of God coming through the garden for His daily visit. Always before they looked forward to this perfect fellowship with their Creator, but now something was different. They still felt sinful and separated, a condition unremedied by their fig-leaf outfits. So they hid among the garden trees.

A few folk handle this fear of nakedness in a different way. Instead of trying to hide, they prefer exposure. They become nudists who extol the benefits of total honesty without distractions or divisions caused by clothing. Everyone is theoretically equal.

When gathered for the weekend in some secluded retreat, millionaires can mix with paupers. Education, culture, and social standing cannot be reflected in a stylish outfit. A nudist has no pockets from which to produce money and no place to easily conceal a weapon. Honesty and openness are supposedly cultivated under these open circumstances. Or so the theory goes. One wonders if these people have confused clothes with sin. The absence of clothes might then represent their muddled attempt to regain a state of innocence. Shed your clothes and rid yourself of sin! Could a complicated subconscious be so simple?

The Bible teaches that everyone of us will stand before God with nothing hidden. Sins long kept secret from others on earth will be revealed. Jesus said,

> Nothing is covered up that will not be revealed, or hidden that will not be known. Therefore whatever you have said in the dark shall be heard in the light, and what you have whispered in private rooms will be proclaimed upon the housetops (Luke 12:2-3).

God does not need to wait until judgment to see our secret sins. Phillips vividly translates Hebrews 4:13 as "No creature has any cover from the sight of God; everything lies naked and exposed before the eyes of him with whom we have to deal."

What a fearful thought! We live naked lives before God. With sins so open and exposed, we have no room for negotiation with God. He knows all. Our position is untenable and hopeless as we stand naked without defense. Surely we shall be separated forever from God.

But wait! Christ intercedes for us. Our nakedness before God is but one of many deserved fears which fail to separate us from the love of Christ. Chalk up another bad condition in which we find the good news still true. Again, we are more than conquerors.

Peril

At thirty-thousand feet the British Airways 747 was cruising far above normal clouds when a dark shadow loomed ahead. That was definitely no ordinary cloud. Not at five miles high!

Pilot Eric Moody had no previous warning about the high-flying peril looming before his plane. A spectacular eruption of a volcano hundreds of miles away was still spewing ash into the air. It was too late to turn. They entered the cloud and were enveloped in darkness.

The yellowish ash clogged and choked all four engines. Within seconds they shut down. Then there was an eerie silence.

Inside the cabin, 139 panic-stricken passengers were engulfed by smoke. Some screamed. Others had to be restrained. Flight attendants checked seat belts and prepared for a crash landing.

Meanwhile, Captain Moody fought desperately at the cockpit controls. His plane was plunging into a steep dive. From thirty-thousand to twenty-five-thousand, and then to twenty-thousand feet.

The pilot managed to skillfully pull his heavy craft into a glide. His only hope was buying time to restart the engines. As an experienced pilot he knew this to be theoretically possible but never before done in a 747. He prayed for a miracle. By now all passengers and crew were praying. Even nonbelievers looked to God in urgent faith for a miracle.

Finally, at eleven-thousand feet one engine coughed and came alive! Then another! Amid cheers and hallelujahs they leveled off and limped toward an emergency landing at the nearest airport.

They made it to Jakarta, Indonesia, where Captain Moody

brought the crippled plane in safely. Everyone rejoiced. They would live!

Since a replacement craft would not arrive until later, their flight was scheduled to resume next morning. Everyone had a free evening in a life which only hours before appeared doomed and without hope. How would they spend that time?

Perhaps a few found quiet places of prayer. Others may have sought churches where they could worship and share their testimonies with others. Those interviewed by news media, however, didn't express any obligation to God. Almost without exception the group took off for a wild night on the town!

Next morning many passengers missed that flight because they were still in a drunken stupor. Others suffered intense hangovers from their celebrations and complained about everything. So much for the answered prayers and miracles graciously given by God. They went back to life as usual.

Let us reconstruct the situation. Is the Christian response different when strapped in a seat of a disabled airliner plunging to destruction below? Perhaps we are more familiar and comfortable with the resource of prayer than others. We are certainly more apt to express our thanksgiving later to God. But the key difference is not before or after peril. It is in the midst of danger that our faith responds with confidence.

With Paul we gladly rejoice: "For I know whom I have believed, and am persuaded that he is able to keep that which I have committed unto him against that day" (2 Tim. 1:12, KJV).

Jesus promised us that we would never be left alone. ". . . and lo, I am with you always, to the close of the age" (Matt. 28:20).

From now to the close of the age includes peril and even the possible or probable end of our lives. When Paul included peril in this Romans 8 list of dangers which ought not separate us from the love of Christ, he spoke from personal experience of "imprisonments, with countless beatings, and often near death" (2 Cor. 11:23).

He had faced danger and found Jesus Christ sufficient for every need. Even the dreaded "forty lashes less one" could not dishearten Paul. The public whippings were reputed to be so severe that forty lashes were fatal. So the intent was a beating right up to the point of death. Five times God's man withstood that vicious punishment, in addition to three public beatings with clubs and one stoning.

Other perils also threatened the missionary. "In journeyings often, . . . in perils of robbers, in perils by mine own countrymen, in perils by the heathen, in perils in the city, in perils in the wilderness, in perils in the sea, in perils among false brethern" (2 Cor. 11:26, KJV).

The point is clear. No threat of imminent peril can dissolve or destroy genuine faith placed in Jesus Christ. We shall persevere. We shall conquer with Christ.

In the early 1870s pastor Horatio Spafford knew God's best blessings. His ministry had flourished, his family was well, and they looked forward to a European trip to visit friends. Then a few days before leaving, their home burned. They lost everything they owned, narrowly escaping alive.

Spafford put his family aboard the French liner *Ville du Havre,* one of the largest and safest ships afloat. He remained behind planning to catch them a few weeks later after details of a new house were arranged.

Tragedy struck again on the high seas as the French ship was accidentally rammed by an English vessel with an iron-plated hull. The liner sank with the terrible loss of 226 people. Mrs. Spafford survived, but her four children were separated in the confusion and drowned. When Spafford learned the news, he left immediately in a state of shock to comfort his wife. His most lonely and difficult moment of that voyage came when the captain pointed to the area off the French coast where his children drowned. With a heavy heart Spafford stared into the deep dark water, then prayed, and wrote his testimony in a hymn:

When peace, like a river, attendeth my way,
When sorrows like sea billows roll;
Whatever my lot, thou hast taught me to say,
It is well, it is well with my soul.

That great hymn of faith expresses so well how it ought to be in time of crisis and peril. In his darkest hour of loss, Spafford discovered that God had not left him alone.

Sword

"Put your sword back into its place; for all who take the sword will perish by the sword" (Matt. 26:52). Even in the moment of danger and death, Jesus warned Peter about the practical consequences of violence. How we need that caution today.

Not that knives and swords are so popular. The average American today is not eager to get a hand bloody with weapons that require direct confrontation. Our violence is less direct but more efficient with firearms and terrorist bombs. Don't forget the family automobiles driven on highways by drunken killers who are probably nice people when sober. Now we can express our rage in violence which kills and maims at a safer distance!

In recent years our youth took some subtle hints from culture to coin the expression: "If it feels good, then do it." Few seem to care if the action is morally wrong. The reasoning goes like this: "Since morality is no longer relevant, who cares? Might as well do it as think about it. Get everything in the open."

That is a dangerous philosophy which has led to a shocking custom in movie theaters. It is now socially acceptable for the crowds to applaud the mayhem and cheer the violence on the silver screen! Gone are the restraints—and so is our safety in streets and in society. Crimes of violence have skyrocketed to an alarming degree.

Our middle-class masses are becoming obsessed with violence, not in the streets but in their sports. Our professional sporting events often resemble the ancient gladiatorial fights when bloodthirsty audiences howled in delight as desperate men fought to the death. The Romans defended that custom as a healthy emotional release for the crowds to vent their latent hostility in a harmless outlet. Thus they satisfied their need for blood in the colosseum rather than in the streets and homes. Or, so they said.

Ridiculous? We hear the same argument today used to sell pornographic literature and violent movies. That is about as logical as trying to put out fire with gasoline! More sin will never still the storms of the sin-sick soul.

Movie makers claim vicarious violence is only harmless fantasy and innocent entertainment. Don't believe that! Our dreams, thoughts, and entertainment are rehearsals for real life. Ultimately, we become what we think. We act as we dream and fantasize. "For as he thinketh in his heart, so is he" (Prov. 23:7, KJV).

What a frightening truth! In my mind and heart I am daily making the mold and accumulating the material for the me of tomorrow. Just as I am what I eat, so I am what I think.

Our government claims to be concerned about safety. You have heard about those regulations which detail page after page of specifications for a commode seat. They ought to focus instead upon the damage caused by R-rated movies.

Some Christians would never dream of going to R-rated films where minds and morals are polluted. Yet they pay to have the same filth enter their homes through cable television which includes X-rated material. Perhaps the government ought to place warning signs on television sets to protect us. "Caution! These movies make strong impressions and eventually cause viewer to act in same ways as portrayed on screen!"

Yes, the older, simpler forms of violence with swords have been replaced by other, more pervasive types of violence. How we need God's guidance today. But how comforting to know the security of being in God's care, even when our world slips into chaos and anarchy.

In 1984 five hardened criminals escaped from the maximum security of a Tennessee prison and provoked a reign of terror across the state. They secured firearms and vowed not to be taken alive. Many residents huddled in fear, hoping they would never meet up with any of those desperate fugitives. People locked their doors and did not venture out alone. They prepared for any eventuality.

Paul Windrow, Sr. in nearby Brownsville thought he was prepared with his forty-five-caliber pistol. When two of the fleeing prisoners came to his backyard, he went for his gun. They killed him instantly. Mrs. Windrow was taken hostage but later released unharmed.

On the same day another concerned citizen, Mrs. Louise Degrafinried, was better prepared. She wasn't about to place her trust in a worldly weapon. When the seventy-three-year-old grandmother saw her husband forced by gunpoint back into their rural home, she did not flinch. Mrs. Degrafinried responded in faith to the fugitive.

"Put your gun down. I'm a Christian woman, and I don't want no violence," she told him as they stood eyeball to eyeball. Then the convict, conscious of a power within her that he could not overcome, meekly obeyed. He laid his shotgun on her sofa.

The most urgent business being settled, the kindly grandmother realized her captive was hungry. She whipped up a country breakfast for the famished fugitive who had not eaten in three days. When the police arrived, the kindly grandmother protected her convert until he could eat and rest a while. She surrendered him to the anxious crowd of lawmen only when she was ready and satisfied for his safety.

What did she say to him? "All I knowed to talk to him about

was Jesus," said Mrs. Degrafinried. "And I did." She talked to a murderer how Jesus warned us that those who live by the sword die by the sword. Violence begets violence.

Yes, we must avoid walking in the violent ways of this world. We should be cautious and prudent. Secure locks are necessary. Yet we ought not cower in the dark paralyzed by fear. Remember that the sword cannot destroy the spirit under Christ's control. "I tell you, my friends, do not fear those who kill the body, and after that have no more that they can do" (Luke 12:4).

Sometimes the sword has power over physical life, but it can never separate us from that which is most important for eternal life. Jesus Christ and His love remain a constant and steady presence in our lives. "My Father, who has given them to me, is greater than all, and no one is able to snatch them out of the Father's hand" (John 10:29).

Part Two: No, Nothing Can Separate Us—Not Even

**Death
Life
Angels
Principalities
Things Present
Things to Come
Powers
Height
Depth**

Death

To Texans of several generations the name Jesse James was familiar. Their Jesse James was not a famous train robber but the faithful state treasurer of Texas whose signature appeared on a billion checks. As a sharp administrator, James brought great efficiency to state government when he realized how much tax money could be saved by volume printing of checks. Texans applauded.

Then Jesse James suddenly died, leaving Texas with problems by the truckload. Literally. In fact, he left enough recently printed checks to fill two semitrailer trucks. Normally those thin slips of paper would have distributed billions of dollars in payrolls and purchases. But no longer. Death had changed wisdom into foolishness.

When the old man died in office, these presigned checks were useless. The original printing bill had cost the state twenty-five thousand dollars, and it took still more tax money for secure disposal of the checks.

All because of death. You see, those familiar checks represented promises to pay. When the person behind the promises died, both paper and promise proved worthless.

Death cancels many a contract. But not so in the case of Jesus Christ who promised us the world. Forever. Then He, too, died.

But what a difference. His death paid for our sins and established for certain the depths of His love toward us. Yet the best part was still to come. Rather than cancel His promises, death helped prove power behind those promises.

"He is not here: for he is risen" (Matt. 28:6, KJV). That was the message of angels left behind in an open tomb for those first witnesses.

No problems here. Rather than dreams destroyed by death, Jesus defeated death. Because Jesus is alive, His promises are good forever. Now we can talk about death with confidence.

How strange that in certain dark periods of history death has been an undiscussed subject. At least we talk about it now. Death and dying were among the first subjects to come out of the closet of a liberated society. No longer is such talk restricted only to churches and funerals. Long past are the days when King Louis XIV of France actually issued a royal decree forbidding any subject related to death to be mentioned in his presence!

Today it seems that no subject is more fascinating. We'll lean closer and listen more intently to hear the last words of a dying soul. In drama the death scene cannot be rivaled for impact. Dying quotes make lively literature in everything from ancient classics to modern bestsellers.

But real life is more awkward for the listener who is asked for help. What can you say to that dying person before he steps from earth into eternity? During World War I an Anglican clergyman volunteered for service as a chaplain with the British. Bishop William Taylor-Smith, chaplain general of the British army, received his application.

Taking a pocket watch from his vest, the chaplain general held it thoughtfully and said: "I am a dying soldier on the battlefield with three minutes to live. What do you have to say to me?"

The minister was confused and could not respond. "Now I have only two minutes to live. What can you tell me to help my soul?"

Finally the minister fumbled for his book of prayers, but the general stopped him. "That will not be enough at a time like this."

Yes, even men of the cloth stammer in the presence of death. It's not easy to find the right words for the dying.

Because dying is so fearful and death is so final, we desperately need help. Authors and publishers who have flooded us with how-to manuals and self-help books have neglected this ultimate need. Typical of the approach of a secular press is one volume purporting to be "the last self-help book you'll ever need." It is a manual on methods of suicide!

Thank God we already have a Book on death and dying which helps us face this last enemy in a more positive approach. No other volume speaks with the authority of "the author and finisher of our faith" who came to earth showing us how to both live and die. In Christ, God in human flesh died for our sins. Death became something not all bad or to be feared because Someone special came back from the grave to comfort us. We are not left in the dark.

Luke reverently records those last words as Jesus died on the cross, "Father, into thy hands I commit my spirit!" (Luke 23:46).

Famous last words! What a good journalist Dr. Luke was—he realized that most people die as they live. What better measure of a person's values, hopes, dreams, faith, and fear than this final test of looking into eternity?

We sadly remember Samson, the strong man who foolishly used his God-given strength for his own pleasures. Samson loved violence. After his tragic downfall caused by his own passion, Samson was blinded and chained. In a final prayer for dying strength, he pushed against the supporting columns of a pagan temple to destroy his enemies, their temple, and himself. His last words? "Let me die with the Philistines" (Judg. 16:30).

How different was the death of Stephen, the first recorded martyr for Jesus. The ugly scene brought out the best in Stephen, who like Jesus died with a prayer of forgiveness on his lips. There was no hatred in his heart. "Lord, lay not this sin to their charge" (Acts 7:60, KJV).

When Sir Walter Raleigh was being led to the death block, his reluctant executioner stammered the instructions. Rather than the customary force required to get a condemned prisoner on his knees, the hooded agent of death found Raleigh willing to place his head on the block. The executioner began offering apologies, but Sir Walter replied: "It matters not how the head lies, provided the heart be right."

Still the trembling executioner hesitated. Kneeling with his head on the block, the usually gentle Raleigh barked a final command. His dying words were, "What dost thou fear? Strike, man!"

So how do you plan to die? Sooner or later each person must deal with death. This ultimate subject is often repressed but never totally ignored.

According to legend, a king once misunderstood his court jester to be making fun of him during a royal performance. In anger the monarch declared the court clown must die. Later, however, he realized his mistake. He had wrongly sentenced an innocent man to death. But worse still, the king sadly remembered that royal decrees could never be changed or canceled. Such was the custom of his time.

The jester was summoned again to the penitent monarch who said: "In consideration of your faithful services and my rash decree, I will grant your dying wish."

The jester thought for a moment and replied, "Does this mean I can choose how I will die?" The king agreed. "Very well, then, I choose to die of old age!"

What a wise and happy choice! If we really must die, let it be of old age in some distant, fuzzy future.

But that is not our choice. No earthly sovereign has the power to promise old age with delayed death. Not even our best medical technology can guarantee life. Despite great strides in lengthening life, the death rate still remains at 100 percent!

Passenger air service today is statistically one of the last places where people die. We are generally safe in the sky, but midway through one flight most passengers knew their plane was in trouble. Soon the captain explained the problem and asked everyone to remain calm. An engine flameout is hard to ignore, however, especially during a storm with a plane losing altitude.

There was no panic but lots of apprehension. Like everyone else, the pastor in seat 22-C used the next few moments to pray. There was something strange about the passenger beside him, however. In the midst of danger and possible death, he seemed cool as a cucumber.

The reverend could not help but be envious. While the crew made crash precautions, this man dozed peacefully. Even crew members were inspired by the example of complete confidence.

Finally, the drama ended happily. Rescue teams with emergency equipment raced beside the crippled plane making a safe but unscheduled landing. Everyone cheered.

The pastor could stand it no longer. He nudged his fellow passenger and asked, "Remarkable! How did you stay so calm?"

"Just a minute," the gentleman replied as he reached into his pocket. He brought out a hearing aid and glasses. "Can't hear a thing without my little helper—and can't see without my glasses. Now what did you say?"

The awful truth dawned on the pastor. The man who appeared so calm and collected was simply ignorant of the danger! When he realized their close brush with death, he really went to pieces! It took three flight attendants to calm him.

Therein lies an unsettling parable about life and death. Ignorance can indeed be bliss, but not forever. Death waits at the end of life. When we realize our ultimate fate, then only genuine faith can comfort us.

John Wesley used to say, "Our people die well." How true for committed Christians! Our advantage is knowing where we go and who we meet after death. We can be the world's only true optimists. Like Francis of Assisi our final farewell to earth can be positive: "Welcome, sister death!" Death will never separate us from the love of Christ.

Life

During our national depression in the 1930s, an elderly lady entered the home office of a Minneapolis insurance company. In her hand was a well-worn policy. She approached the nearest desk to explain her dilemma of no longer being able to pay the monthly premium. Clean but oft-patched clothing testified to her poverty. With no job and faced with the prospect of being evicted from her apartment, she held little hope of continuing the payments.

The clerk recognized this policy was too valuable to let lapse. What did her husband want? It was his policy made out to her benefit.

"My husband? Oh, he has been dead for three years," she remarked sadly. "I want to continue his policy, but I just can't afford it."

Company officials were shocked. They took immediate steps to verify her story and then explained the good news. This was the very situation for which her husband had wisely prepared. As his beneficiary she was due a sizable benefit. They would even refund with interest all that she had paid since his death. The story ended happily.

That's the purpose of life insurance. It ceases to be a liability or cash drain when the policyholder dies. Death makes the difference between premiums paid and benefits bestowed.

Did you know that Jesus Christ made you His beneficiary? He took out the greatest life insurance policy of all time. When Jesus died two-thousand years ago, all sinners became eligible for a wonderful benefit. This policy cancels the consequences of all our sins.

According to the terms of this eternal life insurance agreement, we live because Jesus died. We need only accept the terms as offered. It is a gift of God, not of works. No need to work hard trying to earn eternal life. Jesus paid it all.

And no use trying to deny what He has done. No one can erase history. The death of Jesus and His resurrection happened in real life amid living witnesses. The Jesus story did not emerge from some creative imagination or human longing. As Paul explained to King Agrippa, "For the king knows about these things, and to him I speak freely; for I am persuaded that none of these things has escaped his notice, for this was not done in a corner" (Acts 26:26).

How can something so earthshaking be ignored and even denied? Yet a few nonbelievers take the extreme step of saying they know better. They close their eyes to truth and pretend that two-thousand years of triumphant history by a living Jesus is nothing but a childish fantasy to millions.

How strange that an atheist in the dark can claim that God does not exist while others in the light know God personally. Let the atheist speak only for his own ignorance! In a court of law his testimony is considered worthless. He cannot testify as a witness to what he does not see. A thousand atheists who don't see God cannot counter the testimony of just one person who sees and believes.

Atheists should take a lesson from Thomas after he missed the upper-room appearance of Jesus. Our risen Lord had passed through locked doors into the presence of His disciples, but Thomas found that hard to believe. Yet the doubter had sense enough to limit his argument to his own lack of experience. Rather than denying the possibility of a living Jesus, he sought the same experience his friends had shared. He could believe only when the same evidence was revealed to him personally.

"Unless I see in his hands the print of the nails, and place my finger in the mark of the nails, and place my hand in his side, I will not believe" (John 20:25).

To the eternal credit of "Doubting Thomas," he never went that far. Thomas was there the next time Jesus appeared. He declined to touch the nail prints because he saw and believed. His was a surrendered spirit willing at last to trust his soul to the Man with outstretched hands. After all, the greatest battle is not intellectual debate about God's reality but the struggle to surrender in faith.

Fire had already ravaged out of control through a tenement building before a hook-and-ladder crew arrived. After rescuing several people from burning windows, the firemen maneuvered into position to help a woman hovering on an upper-floor ledge.

A brave fireman strapped himself to the very top of a ladder and extended his arms up toward her. She was only inches above his grasp. He shouted, "Turn loose, lady! I'll catch you!"

A crowd gathered below watching this desperate drama. The panic-stricken woman knew there was no other exit possible, yet she would not leave the temporary security of that ledge. Finally, while the fireman watched helplessly, she was overcome with smoke and fell backward into the flame-filled room.

The fireman returned to the ground visibly shaken. He kept saying, "Why wouldn't she trust me? All she had to do was turn loose. I could have caught her. That's my job. She didn't have to catch me. I would have caught her with these strong hands."

A surrendered spirit—that is the only way we can get out of this world alive. A trust so total that we turn loose to fall into God's hands.

It sounds so simple. Faith is as easy as purposefully falling off a log. Easy, that is, until we try it. The physical body unconsciously reacts. An instinctive reflex condition takes over to reverse the tilt.

Our human nature resists any genuine leap of faith in the same unconscious manner. Part of us—perhaps the mind—understands that decisive action is necessary. But another part of us—the heart—just isn't ready. We hesitate until too late!

Faith in God won't wait until tomorrow. Do it now. We must accept that life insurance offered through Jesus Christ.

"Truly, truly, I say to you, he who hears my word and believes him who sent me, has eternal life; he does not come into judgment but has passed from death to life" (John 5:24).

Angels

Mary Cheatham and Stormie Jones shared a close bond amid the glare of national news in 1985. Their fellowship of suffering originated in hospitals where they were treated for the same rare disease which causes heart-and-liver failure.

When seven-year-old Stormie survived the world's first heart-liver transplant in Pittsburg, seventeen-year-old Mary found encouragement. Now she, too, could hope for life through this pioneer surgery.

Mary's own operation went well, but then the lovely teenager from Texas developed postoperative complications. America wept when Mary Cheatham died during a dramatic attempt to implant yet another heart-lung combination to replace those her body rejected.

Everyone worried then for little Stormie. She was crushed. How would she respond?

"I know Mary is in heaven now," Stormie said softly. "She is a little angel, and I am sure she is watching over everyone, 'specially me.'"

Such a tender thought tugged at heartstrings as the quote flashed across the country. Who would deny a precious seven-year-old her simple, childlike faith?

Yet Stormie's belief in angels falls far short of biblical truth. Somewhere the poor child was never taught the real nature of angels. But who can blame her? Many otherwise well-grounded Christians have only the vaguest idea of angel ranks and ministries. Even more difficult to understand is the danger posed to us from a minority of fallen angels who threaten to separate us from the love of Christ.

Because we generally regard angels (literally "messengers" in both Hebrew and Greek) as positive agents for God, we might be surprised to find angels listed in a negative possibility in this Romans 8:38 list. Along with the writer to the Hebrews, we can ask: "Are they not all ministering spirits sent forth to serve, for the sake of those who are to obtain salvation?" (Heb. 1:14).

To understand why Paul considered some angels to be a possible threat in our relationship to God, we must first understand what angels are in God's realm. Like all living beings, angels were created by God. However, they live and minister in a different dimension from human creatures. They do not marry or have children (Matt. 22:30).

For now angels might be a little higher in some functions and roles, but we are created in the image of God. Unlike those glorious beings, we who are regenerated and delivered from sin will ultimately rule in heaven with God. Paul reminded the Corinthians that we would someday even judge angels (1 Cor. 6:3).

Jesus did not die to redeem sinless angels. All angels are forever fixed in their present state. Their ranks are definitely not being increased by children or adults who die and become angels.

Angels can be classified according to their nature. Most appear to be holy (Mark 8:38) or elect (1 Tim. 5:21). They are called "the angels of God" (John 1:51). Besides ministering around the throne of God, they serve as divine ambassadors to announce glad tidings and carry messages to people on earth. Angels serve as the agents of destruction and judgment at times (Gen. 19:13). They rejoice in the salvation of sinners (Luke 15:10).

Angels serve as our guardians. God has given "his angels charge of you, to guard you in all your ways. On their hands they will bear you up, lest you dash your foot against a stone" (Ps. 91:11-12).

This personal ministry of holy angels for each of us begins early in life. "See that you do not despise one of these little ones; for I tell you that in heaven their angels always behold the face of my Father who is in heaven" (Matt 18:10).

Now back to Paul's implication in Romans 8:38 that angels might threaten to separate us from the love of Christ. Why would some angels try such a terrible thing? Remember that misery loves company! They wish to come between us and Jesus because they are doomed to eternal punishment. "Depart from me, you cursed, into the eternal fire prepared for the devil and his angels" (Matt. 25:41).

This connotation from Jesus presumably predates human history when Satan turned against God and led some other angels astray with him. Jude recounted how these angels "did not keep their own position but left their proper dwelling" (v. 6).

In a dramatic flashback before time began, Revelation 12 describes that original conflict. A vivid glance of heavenly war presents Satan as the dragon with his angels fighting against Michael and his angels. "And the great dragon was thrown down, that ancient serpent, who is called the Devil and Satan, the deceiver of the whole world—he was thrown down to the earth, and his angels were thrown down with him" (v. 9).

Although Satan and his demon angels were cast out of heaven, they continue to wage war in high places and here on earth. We are wise to beware of the evil one. This defeated foe still wins many battles, but the ultimate victory is ours!

We need not fear his power as long as we trust in the greater power of God. "Resist the devil and he will flee from you" (Jas. 4:7) "For he who is in you is greater than he who is in the world" (1 John 4:4).

Paul was right. Angels can never separate us from Christ. "There is no fear in love, but perfect love casts out fear" (v. 18).

Principalities

When actress Grace Kelly married her real-life prince charming in 1956, few Americans knew the location of this tiny principality called Monaco. It mattered little that this entire country on the French Riviera measured scarcely more than one-half square mile in size. The important thing was the dream fulfilled. The girl next door grew into a beautiful lady, became a famous film star, and then married the handsome Prince Rainier.

That media event offered a rare opportunity for the English term *principality* to be used in its earthly meaning as a political territory or jurisdiction of a human prince. But this word also expresses a biblical concept applied to a heavenly sphere of authority among the angels. The Greek word *arche* is variously translated ruler, authority, or principality. Satan rules or exercises authority over other angels in his principality.

When Paul listed principalities as a possible threat to separate us from the love of Jesus, he was developing a thought he previously raised with the danger of angels. Scholars have suggested many possible relationships here, but for our purpose we know that principalities are more a sphere than a place.

Paul was the only New Testament writer to employ this word. His most memorable yet mysterious use of the term is found in a warning to the Ephesians of another worldly danger.

> For we are not contending against flesh and blood, but against the principalities, against the powers, against the world rulers of this

present darkness, against the spiritual hosts or wickedness in the heavenly places (Eph. 6:12).

In his Letter to the Colossians, Paul mentioned that God through Christ "disarmed the principalities and powers and made a public example of them, triumphant over them in him" (Col. 2:15).

That sounds as if these other worldly rulers once tried to exercise authority far outside God's control. But Paul clearly emphasized how they were an original part of God's creation (Col. 2:15). Indeed, Christ "is the head of all principality and power" (Col. 2:10, KJV).

How comforting to know that no matter how powerful a ruler or how important a principality which might be arrayed against us, we are kept safe through Jesus Christ. No earthly power or other worldly authority can separate us here on earth from the love of Jesus Christ.

Things Present

Even with competition from radio and television, newspapers are holding their own in the race to keep people informed about what's going on in our world. Daily newspapers are current and describe "things present."

In 1871 all the civilized world clamored for news about Dr. David Livingstone. The famous missionary was long overdue and presumed lost on his third trip into Africa.

In America the *New York Herald* wanted desperately to beat its English competition, so it commissioned Henry M. Stanley for the search. Restless, impulsive, a religious cynic, and somewhat unstable idealist—this soldier of fortune had fought in the American

Civil War at different times for both sides! He also had a nose for news and considerable journalistic skills.

Every schoolchild remembers Stanley's immortal quote when he finally found the explorer in darkest Africa: "Dr. Livingstone, I presume?"

Not so well remembered today is the remarkable influence of the old missionary upon the young adventurer. Stanley, the impatient nonbeliever, spent four months with Livingstone in central Africa. He was forever changed.

His journalistic career was ensured. All the world read his dispatches and now recognized his name. But somehow Stanley sensed something missing in his old life-style. The strange, quiet warmth of Livingstone intrigued him.

Here was a saint who possessed what Stanley had always denied was real. Livingstone demonstrated a gift of living, not in the past or in the future but joyfully in the present. Stanley became a Christian, saying: "I was converted by him, although he had not tried to do it."

Stanley left his own past behind and decided to go into a new direction for the future. He cast his lot in life with Livingstone. When Livingstone died in Africa, Stanley continued the work of exploration which laid the foundation for Christian missions in that dark continent. He had learned to live one day at a time.

Life in the present tense. A thought-provoking quip reminds us that "Today is the tomorrow you worried about yesterday. It's not so bad, is it? So enjoy today!"

Rather than enjoy today as the time of our lives, we moderns are more likely to fret about it. We occupy ourselves with measuring and recording time. Computer technology and atomic science have broken time into micro particles with strange names and as small as one billionth of a second. Now we can't even agree on a common standard for time.

The traditional basis for time—called solar time—measures how long it takes earth to rotate on its axis. Scientists, however, favor atomic clocks based upon the frequency of electromagnetic waves given off by atoms or molecules. Normally the two processes are identical, but occasionally the earth rotates in irregular patterns that can interrupt all our precise calculations. Then something has to give. Atomic clocks must be slowed down or speeded up in matching adjustments. Scientists moan, but the annual correction is usually made on New Year's eve.

How much time and how often are we changing the clocks? Don't panic, but all the fuss is about one second per year! For 1984 officials at the United States Naval Observatory in Washington refused to adjust the master clock for the traditional leap second. No one could explain why it was unnecessary. Consistency was dealt yet another blow in the eyes of time-conscious experts.

God's Word contains nearly a thousand references to time in its different human perspectives—days, months, years, seasons, harvests. "For everything there is a season, and a time for every matter under heaven" (Eccl. 3:1).

But these frequent references to time seldom stress quantity. The holy measurement most often made is in terms of life quality with an emphasis upon present tense. "Behold, now is the acceptable time; behold, now is the day of salvation" (2 Cor. 6:2).

While the children of Israel wandered in the wilderness between Egyptian slavery and the Promised Land, manna fell from heaven to sustain them. But it never lasted beyond the next day as God taught them to depend daily upon Him. In the same spirit of things present, Jesus taught us to pray: "Give us this day our daily bread" (Matt. 6:11).

Past and future do not matter nearly as much as this present time. We Christians have been accused of being preoccupied with "pie in the sky by and by." But our faith—properly exercised—takes place in the here and now. The past lives only in our memories while the future exists as hope. "This is the day the Lord has made; let us rejoice and be glad in it" (Ps. 118:24).

Paul gave the forgiven past only a backward glance ("forgetting what lies behind") and trusted the future with his best effort ("straining forward to what lies ahead"). But his emphasis shared with the Philippians in that classic statement of Christian goals centered upon the things present. "But one thing I do, forgetting what lies behind and straining forward to what lies ahead, I press on [present tense] toward the goal for the prize of the upward call of God in Christ Jesus" (Phil. 3:13-14).

Our Lord Jesus comforted us with assurances known as the Beatitudes or blessings which began His Sermon on the Mount. While we sometimes see them as promises for the future (which they indeed are), we must note the true emphasis upon the present. Nine times Jesus began "Blessed *are* . . ." in the present tense. The poor in spirit, those who mourn, the meek, and other sufferers in faith are all blessed *now* as well as later (Matt. 5:1-11).

Paul echoed this same emphasis in our theme passage of Romans 8. In verse 37 things present is presented as a possible challenge to faith, but in "all these things we are [present tense again!] more than conquerors through him who loved us."

Things To Come

A fable from India describes a mouse living in total fear of the cat. He cringed at the thought of what might happen should that cat ever catch him.

Finally the Creator could stand it no longer. Taking pity on the poor mouse, He promised a change. Presto! The mouse became a cat.

Now, the mouse inside a cat feared the dog. He was no better off than before, so God went another step further and let him become a dog. But as a dog he feared the tiger. Then God let him be a tiger only to hear the same whimpering fear. Now he was afraid of the hunter.

Finally God said, "Be a mouse again. I can't help you become something you aren't if you are so afraid of what you might become."

Too often we act like that mouse. We let our fears overshadow our faith and take a worry trip that gets us nowhere but depressed and down. And almost all those worries are about tomorrow's troubles.

Jesus warned us about a negative spirit dwelling upon things to come. Today's burdens we can bear with the help of God, but not if we borrow from the troubles of tomorrow. "Therefore do not be anxious about tomorrow, tomorrow will be anxious for itself. Let the day's own trouble be sufficient for the day" (Matt. 6:34).

Have you ever noticed how in good times our interest in prophecy wanes? When happy or busy, we aren't as curious about things to come.

During the "Gay Nineties" and the "Roaring Twenties," America rejoiced in economic prosperity. With the exception of the World-War-I era, the national mood was upbeat. Prophetic interest waned. Yet uncertain times often create resurging interest in prophecy.

Beginning with the 1960s we witnessed the beginning of some very negative trends—rampant inflation, rebellious youth, economic displacement caused by automation and cybernation, public assassinations of our leaders, threat of nuclear annihilation, and a rise of the occult. Those uncertain times spurred renewed interest in prophecy. Some seers began issuing vague pronouncements about politics and famous people. Although consistently wrong in specific predictions, some seers are still regarded highly by the American public. Perhaps it is because they claim their ability is a gift from God.

Prophets of doom sprang up everywhere. Our worldwide economy was destined to crash, they said. Better put your money in gold and stockpile plenty of food! Survivalism assumed a new and ominous meaning with bomb shelters and guns to protect one's family from panic-stricken neighbors who had unwisely failed to prepare for that coming chaos.

In the religious corner, Christians discovered books about prophetic subjects. Daniel and Revelation became popular texts for preaching and prophecy conferences.

What is the gist of their message? It was almost as negative as the secular prophets. Citing obscure verses and presenting many strange scenarios, these negative harbingers have said: "You think the world is in a bad shape now? You haven't seen anything yet!"

Why do we so fear the future? Not all things to come are negative. Paul looked into the future with hope. God is in charge. No matter what our problems of this present time, they will pale in the glory that is to come. "I consider the sufferings of this present time are not worth comparing with the glory that is to be revealed to us" (Rom. 8:18).

D. L. Moody talked about the two ways Christians can travel toward heaven. We can go first class or second class. Second class is found in Psalm 56:3 which says: "What time I am afraid, I will trust in thee" (KJV).

First class is far better. The famous evangelist cited Isaiah 12:2. "I will trust, and will not be afraid." That's first class all the way! The things to come in life will not get us down.

We Christians can be positive about the future because we've read the end of the book. We know that everything turns out well with God.

As head football coach at the University of Texas, Daryl Royal preferred a running game. No one was more pessimistic about the pass play. Royal often said: "When you put the ball into the air, only three things can happen. And two of them are bad!"

In the museum apartment of Thomas Carlyle in London, visitors are shown a soundproof room which the great poet and writer had designed for his own purposes. He wanted to study, write, and sleep in perfect peace. Carlyle, however, never reckoned on his neighbor's rooster whose shrill morning ritual could easily penetrate those thick walls to interrupt his privacy. When the poet complained, his neighbor casually dismissed the problem by replying: "Toward daybreak a rooster will be a rooster. But after all, he crows only a couple times each morning. What could be so bad about that?"

In frustration verging on tears, Carlyle answered: "But you don't know how terrible it is for me lying awake all night just *waiting* for that old bird to crow!"

Too often we are just as guilty in dreading things to come. We worry ourselves sick about something that is unimportant or probably won't happen anyway.

I was once pastor to a beloved but pitiful church member who constantly complained of various illnesses. I was generally reluctant to ask, "How are you?" She usually told me anyway! But on one occasion she looked so fit, I took a chance and asked how she fared.

She said, "Oh, Brother Pastor, this is just terrible. I feel better today than I have felt in years—but I know that it won't last. I'm so worried I will get sick again that I can't think about anything else."

When Paul looked into the future, he saw great things ahead for the believers in Jesus. "I consider the sufferings of this present time are not worth comparing with the glory that is to be revealed to us" (Rom. 8:18).

Powers

In 1781 Sir William Herschel made the first discovery of a new planet since ancient astronomers began charting the skies. Our sun's seventh planet, Uranus, was found wandering in the far, distant reaches of our solar system.

Herschel studied the faint image for months and then plotted its exact course for the next one-hundred years. What a brilliant feat in that era before computers!

As the years rolled on, later astronomers realized that the new planet was not moving as predicted. A careful reexamination of Herschel's original calculations produced no error.

Somewhere out there, far beyond their sight, an unseen power was pulling Uranus from its orbit. The astronomers suspicioned another planet.

Still later the riddle was studied by mathematicians Adams and LeVerrier. Using Herschel's original figures, they described key details about the mystery planet on the other side of Uranus.

Sure enough, when better telescopes were finally designed, a new planet fitting that description was discovered. It was named Neptune.

Funny thing about the size, speed, and location of Neptune. Although no one had ever seen the planet, much was known about it. No surprises.

Every key fact about the hidden Neptune had already been postulated by how its invisible power had affected Uranus. No one had to see Neptune to believe its existence. Power can be persuasive!

In the New Testament the word for *power* in its singular form occurs often and is usually associated with divine authority. It is a positive concept. The disciples were promised power "when the Holy Spirit has come upon you; and you shall be my witnesses" (Acts 1:8).

And power they received! A small, determined group fanned out with unusual force that was obviously heaven sent for heaven-bound believers. Christians were filled with power from above. It was an explosive force summarized by the Greek word *dunamis*.

Swedish chemist Alfred Nobel understood some earthly principles of power when he patented a mixture of gunpowder and nitroglycerin. Three years later in 1866 he created another powerful substance so unique that a new word seemed necessary. That is when he seized upon this Greek transliteration of *dunamis* for what we now call *dynamite*.

Nobel was never a violent man. He had envisioned dynamite as a peaceful tool to clear stumps for farms or for road building. Just how totally different the world viewed his contribution to civilization was revealed when he opened his newspaper one morning.

The headline screamed "Alfred Nobel Dead." An article subtitled "Dynamite King Dies" described him as "the Merchant of Death" and "Inventor of Destruction." They were wrong, of course, about his death. Apparently another Alfred Nobel had died, and a reporter eager for a scoop rushed his story over the wires too soon.

Yet the account caused much self-examination in Nobel's heart. Was that how people really thought of him? The situation so bothered him that something had to be done. Nobel took his fortune and dedicated it to honoring great men and women who advanced the cause of peace through nonviolent fields of medicine and physics. Through the Nobel peace prize today, positive power is encouraged.

When does power become negative? In the New Testament we sense something wrong any time the word occurs in its plural form. "Powers" can invoke a mysterious connotation, especially when connected with principalities.

In our Romans 8:38 list of fears, the word for *principalities* is placed immediately after angels. Then the term for powers is located between the classifications of time (things present and things to come) and space (height and depth). Perhaps by separating principalities from powers, Paul was reminding us that the seductive temptations of powers do not always come dressed in dark, sinister garb.

According to an old saying, "Power corrupts, and absolute

power corrupts absolutely." Much of the history of this world has been written in blood and tears caused by once-benevolent rulers later turned evil by powers unchallenged and unchecked. They didn't start out that way.

The world's clearest example of multiple powers gone bad is Satan, the highest angel who rebelled against the Creator. Paul warned about the deceptive tactics of this eternal enemy who often disguises his dark, destructive powers. "And no wonder, for even Satan disguises himself as an angel of light" (2 Cor. 11:14).

Of these powers we ought to beware. Satanic forces seek to separate us from Christ. Evil powers arrayed against us would be overwhelming except for the constant, abiding presence of a greater power within us. "Because greater is he that is in you, than he that is in the world" (1 John 4:4, KJV).

Height

Phobias. Among these persistent, irrational, and unrealistic fears, acrophobia—fear of heights—is probably the most common. Even the most confident and emotionally healthy individuals occasionally experience an acrophobic nightmare with that dreaded sensation of falling from some high place.

Perhaps Paul had this fear in mind when he included height in his list of forces which threaten unsuccessfully to separate us from the love of Christ. Others suggest his reference to height and depth were simply random fears representing space or distance as a final example of many general fears. The Greek term *hupsōma* means high thing or high place.

In making travel arrangements for a revival to be preached in a distant state, a pastor discovered the only convenient transportation was by air. He disliked flying. In fact, he feared even to set foot in an airplane. His deacon chairman was chiding him in a good-natured way for lack of faith. After all, didn't Jesus promise to always be with him? The frightened pastor had a ready response. He countered that this promise didn't count up high: "But *lo,* I am with you always!"

"Who shall ascend the hill of the Lord? And who shall stand in his holy place? He who has clean hands and a pure heart" (Ps. 24:3). "Praise the Lord! Praise the Lord from the heavens, praise him in the heights!" (Ps. 148:1).

Mountains have always been associated with high points of inspiration. We remember Mount Carmel where Elijah proved God more powerful than the false gods of Baal. The psalmist associated the heights of the hills with the help of God. "I will lift up my eyes to the hills. From whence does my help come? My help comes from the Lord, who made heaven and earth" (Ps. 121:1).

Our Lord's greatest collection of truth is contained in what we call the Sermon on the Mount. He often took His disciples unto the hills for meditation and training. The heights were inspiring. Jesus was revealed most clearly on the mount of transfiguration.

But the heights are also areas of dominion for "spiritual wickedness in high places" (Eph. 6:12, KJV). Satan is described as "the prince of the power of the air" (Eph. 2:2) He once boasted in his heart:

> I will ascend to heaven; above the stars of God;
> I will set my throne on high;
> I will sit in the mount of assembly in the far north;
> I will ascend above the heights of the clouds;
> I will make myself like the Most High (Isa. 14:13-14).

In trying to counterfeit qualities of the Most High, Satan claims the heights here on earth. His disciples locate their altars in the high places. During the dark days of apostasy and spiritual decline in ancient Israel, many of God's people started worshiping the false gods of Canaan. King Asa of Judah tried to direct the people back unto God. "He put away the male cult prostitutes out of the land, and removed all the idols that his fathers had made." Yet the historian notes sadly in the same account "But the high places were not taken away" (1 Kings 15:12, 14).

The spiritual battles for control of hearts and minds were fought in the hills where high places of worship unto Satan's powers were centered. Good kings like Hezekiah and Josiah tore down the evil altars, but evil leaders like Manasseh returned to the abominable practices.

> For he rebuilt the high places which Hezekiah his father had destroyed; and he erected altars for Baal, and made an Asherah, as Ahab king of Israel had done, and worshiped all the host of heaven, and served them (2 Kings 21:3).

In that third and most powerful temptation of Jesus, the devil chose a location comfortable to satanic power.

> Again, the devil took him to a very high mountain, and showed him all the kingdoms of the world and the glory of them; and he said to him, "All these I will give you, if you will fall down and worship me" (Matt. 4:8-9).

Yes, the view was inspiring. Earthly kingdoms were majestic with glory as seen from that high mountain. But it was not the view that seemed so inviting. Don't miss the significance of that high place where the evil one appears to be much at home. How tempting to forget the sufferings of a cross and the darkness of death. Satan was offering an easy route to second-class success if only Jesus would acknowledge a demonic dominion. In that highest of high places, Jesus would have no earthly equal. Just fall down in worship of the devil as others have done.

Jesus held firm and resisted that final temptation in a high place. Rather than fight evil with evil, our Lord accepted the burden of all human sin in His body. He took the worst Satan could lay on

Him in death, but God's power was greater and higher. God raised Jesus from the dead and

> made him sit at his right hand in the heavenly places, far above all rule and authority and power and dominion, and above every name that is named . . . and he has put all things under his feet (Eph. 1:20-21).

Look up! There is nothing higher than Jesus. He is already seated at the right hand of God in the heavenly places. Nothing looks down on Jesus. He is at the very top. And because He is there, we need not fear any height.

Depth

What is the most popular form of mass transportation in terms of total distance? Not cars, planes, or trains which crisscross the world. In sheer numbers all those mechanical marvels combined do not move as many people daily as the common elevator!

It is the only transportation system in America offering a free ride for passengers. And they are safe. Based upon total passenger trips, elevators are a thousand times safer than your family car.

Who invented this miracle of upward mobility? Not the Russians. Nor the Americans. The Roman architect, Vitruvius, described a similar contraption a century before Christ. It seems that ropes, pulleys, and lifts were ancient tools even then.

The elevator finally made modern skyscrapers practical. Builders had long possessed the skills and materials necessary to build in the sky, but few tenants would climb above four flights. The solution came in the 1850s with safe elevators developed by Elisha Otis.

Contrary to popular belief, the longest elevator ride has never been in the Empire State Building or any other skyscraper. The key is depth with the honor going to a South African gold mine over a mile deep. That elevator door opens not unto a beautiful view but unto total darkness and almost unbearable heat.

Imagine the terror to those passengers going deep down should the elevator fail. All life below depends upon a guaranteed return trip. There is no other way out. Even the most terrified miner knows he must trust that small box. He has no choice but to enter and patiently await his upward lift to life above. "Out of the depths I cry to thee, O Lord! Lord hear my voice!" (Ps. 130:1).

That basically describes our situation here on earth. Left alone to our own wits, we are helpless with no hope of getting off this planet alive. "They go down again to the depths: their soul is melted because of trouble. They reel to and fro, and stagger like a drunken man, and are at their wit's end" (Ps. 107:26-27, KJV).

By tradition, sailors have been most fearful of the dark depths below. During Spain's colonization of Central and South America, many ships sank with tragic loss of life. Records indicate the most dangerous passage was by heavily armed galleons traveling from the New World back to Spain.

These ships were heavily loaded with valuables looted from temples and royal treasuries. Claiming these spoils of war was easy compared to getting them back to the mother country. Some of the best commercial captains could not be trusted with such treasure, so loyalty and rank were more important than ability. These naval officers were not always familiar with Caribbean weather and shipping hazards.

A common pattern developed when the ships riding too low due to heavy treasure ran into bad weather or hidden reefs. First, the rats fled their flooded compartments below. Then up came the soldiers assigned to guard the valuables being transported. Many soldiers jumped overboard in panic and soon drowned.

A few, clear-minded survivalists sought any type flotation device. They ripped up wood or chose boxes and barrels according to well-planned drills.

Many, however, spent their last moments hoarding a fortune now unguarded below. They filled their pockets with wealth only to be inevitably dragged to the depths below by the heavy weight of gold and silver valuables. Greed is a heavy burden to bear in a watery grave.

Life can be a frightening experience even in the best of times. Always ahead in the dim future is that final stage likened to a leap into death's darkness. Yet there is no hole so deep, no pit so dark, where Jesus Christ will not accompany us. He knows the way because He has been there before. Paul reminded us that Jesus "descended into the lower parts of the earth" (Eph. 4:9).

When Jesus conquered death and came back from His own grave, He demonstrated lordship over our last enemy. He guaranteed our own safe passage. Some day He is returning for us who belong to Him, and we will be caught up in the air. Up and away! Jesus is our only way out, so we will not be afraid.

> For the Lord himself shall descend from heaven with a shout, with the voice of the archangel, and with the trump of God: and the dead in Christ shall rise first. Then we which are alive and remain shall be caught up together with them in the clouds, to meet the Lord in the air: and so shall we ever be with the Lord. Wherefore comfort one another with these words (1 Thess. 4:16-18).

Part Three: Nor Anything Else in All Creation

A problem in beginning any detailed list is knowing where to stop. As mentioned in the introduction, Paul left out many significant fears that we might think capable of separating us from the love of Christ. But the list is now made all-inclusive by this sweeping phrase "nor anything else in all creation" (Rom. 8:39). Nothing is left out. No loopholes exist. All creation is considered and judged incapable of conquering us. We are super conquerors!

In this final section we examine further categories which the apostle could have included as possible wedges between Christ and the believer. Many are obviously negative, some positive, and others neither. But each provides a possibility of victory.

Survival Kit

The spring fishing trip had been everything any boy could desire, so both father and son happily prepared for the return trip over the Canadian wilderness. Then tragedy struck. Their light plane developed mechanical problems and crashed twelve miles north of Flin Flon, Manitoba.

Walter Sedor's father died on impact. Somehow this eight-year-old boy climbed out before the plane burned. He patiently waited for help while search planes from the Royal Canadian Air Force crisscrossed seventy-thousand square miles. No luck. The search party gave up.

After fifteen days an alert pilot for a commercial airline finally sighted a starving survivor near some charred wreckage. It was Walter. Rescue teams arrived within hours. Although weakened by the ordeal, Walter lived.

The experience offered much irony. Whether through shock or good sense, Walter had remained close to the plane. Otherwise searchers probably would have never found him.

Perhaps the crash site offered comfort to the boy. The remains of his dad rested in that wreckage. But just a few feet away laid a box with physical comfort inside. It had been thrown clear of the impact, but for some strange reason Walter was never curious enough to check the contents.

It turned out that Walter should never have gone hungry. His father had earlier provided food in a survival kit containing twenty-four days of emergency rations!

Too many of us are like that child. Unaware of God's provision for us, we stumble in the emotional and spiritual wildernesses of this life. Too often we overlook a survival kit from God—a Book. Inside waits an invitation to try the Bread of Life which can satisfy any soul hungry for things spiritual.

Practically everyone in the Western world has such a Book available. Millions of copies are given as gifts by family, friends, organizations, and churches. But this survival kit must be opened and used before blessings abound. So read it and thrive!

It is written,

> Man shall not live by bread alone, but by every word that proceeds from the mouth of God (Matt. 4:4).
>
> For the bread of God is that which comes down from heaven, and gives life to the world. Jesus said unto them, "I am the bread of life; he who comes to me shall not hunger, and he who believes in me shall never thirst" (John 6:33, 35).

Secrets

How would *you* like to find a million dollars? Two men in Philadelphia stopped their battered old car along a busy street to examine a yellow cart on wheels which had rolled to the curb. Inside they found $1.2 million carelessly lost from an armored truck.

The shipment of used hundred-dollar bills from a Federal Reserve Bank was headed for casinos in Atlantic City, New Jersey. A witness reported the joyful pair grabbed the bags of unmarked money and sped off.

Their joy was short-lived. The old adage "Losers weepers, finders keepers" did not apply in this case. News media spread the word that the money was legally classified as "unattended," not lost. The true owner was the lax security firm which lost it.

The detective in charge of a city-wide search was confident.

Although he had only a vague description and no license plates, Captain Robert Eichler promised to find the men and recover at least a portion of the money.

Now how could anyone be so confident? He explained that clues weren't necessary to solve this case. He could count on human nature that can't keep a secret.

It works like this. Most ordinary people cannot resist spending the windfall. Family, friends, or fellow workers notice the sudden prosperity and become suspicious. A loose word here, a boast there, and someone close puts two and two together.

Now a secret like that is too hot to handle. The friend will either report the thieves and claim a fifty-thousand-dollar reward, or he will demand a cut of the loot. If he does join the party, someone else will soon make the same deduction and want a share. Sooner or later, coconspirators get angry, jealous, or greedy. The police receive a tip, and the party is over.

That is exactly how the plot unfolded. The detective was right on target. Within a week the two men plus one later participant were in custody.

Good news just cannot be kept quiet. A more positive instance occurred while Jerusalem languished under Syrian seige in the days of Elisha. God's people were starving.

Four lepers in the countryside reasoned among themselves that they had little to lose by begging bread from the Syrians. Trembling, they approached the camp which turned out to be mysteriously deserted. Earlier the Lord had made these enemy soldiers hear the sound of chariots, horses, and a great army. They fled, leaving great stores of food, supplies, silver, gold, and garments.

The first response of the happy lepers was to gorge themselves on food. Then they carried off precious booty and hid it. Finally, they realized their discovery must be shared.

> We are not doing right. This day is a day of good news; if we are silent and wait until the morning light, punishment will over-

take us; now therefore come, let us go and tell the king's household (2 Kings 7:9).

Good news that sensational might as well be shouted from the rooftops. Sooner or later, that secret will be known anyway.

Rewards

The Saratoga Battlefield was the place where Americans fought for freedom during the Revolutionary War. Four officers distinguished themselves as heroes in that battle and inspired grateful citizens to promise a massive monument in their honor. That would be the first order of business for peacetime.

Some years later they completed the monument, but with only three statues. A vacant space was left where the fourth hero would have been honored. This handsome officer from a distinguished family was not included for obvious reasons. General Benedict Arnold had turned traitor.

Where did he go wrong? Not in basic battlefield ability or courage. Arnold inspired confidence in his soldiers and showed no fear while in danger. His later moral failure surfaced not in combat dangers but in civilian pleasures. General Arnold loved lavish living with fine clothes and high society entertainment which kept him deeply in debt.

Saratoga's fourth hero brooded that fame and honor paid poor wages. He was bitter and broke. When his promotion to major general was delayed while younger officers received those coveted stars, Arnold decided to even the score on the salary issue. He would let the enemy provide his rewards.

The British army gladly paid for his services as a spy who delivered military secrets. Then they kept a polite distance from him thereafter. After all, who can trust a traitor? Benedict Arnold lived the rest of his life in regret and died in lonely exile in the British Isles.

Historians generally agree that Arnold deserved further promotions if one considered only his abilities. On the other hand, his haughty and cavalier attitudes created resentment with others equally qualified. In their final evaluation, his superiors were more concerned with character than ability. Unfortunately, Arnold's later treason proved that he was indeed an opportunist more loyal to himself than to his country.

Loyal soldiers do not count costs or maneuver to even the score. After King Saul turned away from God, the Lord rejected him and sent Samuel to anoint David as the next king. Remarkably, the young man displayed a patient trust in God's timing. As long as Saul lived, David remained loyal to his king.

When driven from Jerusalem by a jealous Saul, David did not resist. He refused to fight back even after Saul tried repeatedly to kill him. Although everyone else believed that God had delivered the vengeful king into David's hand, the young hero would not strike the Lord's anointed. His promotion to the throne came only when God acted.

We are called by God to be soldiers of the cross. He expects our faithful service and complete obedience in that role. Sometimes others may be blessed with promotions which seem undeserved. No matter. How God deals with another servant is no concern of ours. Our loyalty does not depend upon rewards either to ourselves or others.

Some of our Lord's teachings and parables are hard to understand. Others are simple but hard to accept. In this latter category, Jesus compared Kingdom rewards to those given by an employer for day laborers in his vineyard. Some he hired early and they worked all day long. Others came at various times later in the day including some hired just an hour before quitting time. So far no problem.

But then came payoff. Everyone received the same wages—equal pay for unequal work! Those who toiled twelve hours resented a full day's wages given to the one-hour helpers, and we tend to agree with them. Yet Jesus made it plain that another servant's reward is none of our business!

> But he replied to one of them, "Friend, I am doing you no wrong; did you not agree with me for a denarius? Take what belongs to you, and go; I choose to give to this last as I give to you. Am I not allowed to do what I choose with what belongs to me? Or do you begrudge my generosity?" (Matt. 20:13-15).

Yes, most of us do begrudge God's generosity, unless that generosity is to us alone! We identify more with the older son than the prodigal son. Why should God reward a Johnny-come-lately when we were faithful all along? While others sowed wild oats, we labored in God's vineyard. Doesn't faithfulness count for something? Or so the human spirit wants to rationalize. But true faith knows better and trusts further.

> Therefore do not pronounce judgment before the time, before the Lord comes, who will bring to light the things now hidden in darkness and will disclose the purposes of the heart. Then every man will receive his commendation from God (1 Cor. 4:5).

Disease Defeated

During the darkest days of the depression in the 1930s, many unemployed city dwellers envied Southern farmers who were better accustomed to poverty. Poor farmers could at least grow their own garden foods in that warmer climate.

Yet Southerners had their own afflictions. In 1932 an outbreak of infantile paralysis spread fear among parents of stricken children. The dreaded disease respected no race, color, or class.

Finally in December of that year newspapers announced in bold headlines a new hope. A humble little scientist in the backwoods of Alabama had developed a highly successful treatment. Word spread like wildfire. Soon hundreds of parents were making a pilgrimage to Tuskegee Institute seeking Dr. George Washington Carver.

What was his cure? Just plain peanut oil. After a brief visit and examination, Carver personally rubbed this oil into the leg muscles of each child. The results were startling.

Medical records indicate that of the 250 cases he treated, every child showed definite progress. Many were completely cured.

Physicians were intrigued. Could peanut oil become the next miracle medicine? It was an exciting thought, but medical sleuths simply had no funds for serious investigation.

Although researchers were never able to isolate the curative properties of peanut oil, the statistics could not be denied. Besides, no one was eager to contradict Carver. This brilliant, self-educated pioneer had already proven experts wrong with his revolutionary discoveries about the peanut. Medical leaders adopted a wait-and-see attitude.

Gradually the disease subsided and interest shifted to more urgent research. The entire episode faded into the past to be remembered only by grateful parents and curious historians.

Today we still wonder about Dr. Carver's cure. Many observers believed the secret rested in those gentle black hands which administered a therapeutic message. Perhaps it was a charismatic cure through a magnetic personality which inspired confidence to cure oneself.

Others with deeper wisdom recognized a great power beyond Carver. These healings reflected the power of God.

Dr. Carver knew much about botany, chemistry, medicine, and human nature. But, as he often pointed out, all knowledge comes from God who allows men to study and learn the secrets of His creation. Carver's favorite method of research, therefore, depended upon a prayerful attitude and dependence upon God.

Evidently, the peanut oil provided no more medical properties than olive oil used in ancient healings. The substance chosen for anointing oil was not as important as prayer.

Tennyson said it well. "More things are wrought by prayer/ Than this world dreams of." Carver practiced it. And we who base our faith in Jesus Christ understand it.

> Is any among you sick? Let him call for the elders of the church, and let them pray over him, anointing him with oil in the name of the Lord; and the prayer of faith will save the sick man, and the Lord will raise him up (Jas. 5:14-15).

Stewardship

Sam Houston was a man's man long before the modern macho trend became fashionable. Like other rough men molded by the frontier, he knew how to fight, gamble, drink, curse, and kill. He lived in a violent era when life was cheap.

Those early Texans were not against God. If the women, children, and preachers wanted to believe in the Almighty, that was fine with them. Christians were handy to have around for burial prayers. Real men, however, were usually too busy for religion.

But times change, and men mellow. After the Texans won their war for independence from Mexico, schools and churches sprang up everywhere. Society settled down and communities began to flourish. As they grew older, those adventurous men began taking more interest in spiritual matters. And so did the general.

Houston's wife, a devout Baptist, prayed for years that Sam

would join the church. The Texas hero had long claimed to be a believer, but baptism and church membership were not easy disciplines for him to accept.

Finally came the time when the senior statesman of the new republic surrendered. Vowing to go all the way with God and become a Baptist, he met with the congregation at the river for baptism.

"General," the minister said, "I suggest you take off that watch and chain. You'll ruin it if you get it wet."

"Thank you, I will," Houston said handing the piece to a friend.

"And, General, perhaps you had better hand him your wallet, too."

"No, I believe not, Pastor. I'm afraid it needs baptizing, too."

Amen! Even before his baptism, Sam Houston understood the concept of Christian stewardship. Not that God wants just our soul or just our silver. He wants all of us. How appropriate that the man who had held out so long from God should have his billfold baptized. A wet wallet became a witness to Sam Houston's new dedication unto God.

Having waited so long, the General didn't waste time in taking a stewardship stand for God. What a contrast to many church members today who are so casual in financing God's kingdom of faith. They may give a special offering when occasionally challenged, but they do not practice unconditional tithing. They miss the joy of disciplined faith which trusts God to supply every need "according to his riches in glory in Christ Jesus" (Phil. 4:19).

The Greater Plan

"Go West, young man." To one Easterner from New Jersey, that command was no casual matter. It was a medical order from his physician who believed the dry, Western states would cure John B. Stetson's body of "consumption" (tuberculosis).

The young man reluctantly left the comforts of home and joined a Pike's Peak expedition. He was cautioned to rest often and keep his head covered. While the physical exhaustion of the trip probably canceled any climatic benefits, the Western sojourn later changed Stetson. And Stetson was the one who changed the American hat styles.

While camped out under the stars, his companions on that trip had commented upon the need for cloth to make more tents. Stetson told them about a new process called felting which turned fur into cloth. His new friends laughed at him.

Undaunted, Stetson demonstrated the procedure by molding a bit of fur into a much-needed hat. Besides protecting his frail body against the elements, it later made him a tidy profit when a cowboy paid five dollars for his creation.

Years passed and Stetson returned to Philadelphia in good health but poor finances. What could he do to make a living? Then he remembered the hat from his sickly youth.

In 1865 he began making a wide-brimmed, felt hat with a high crown which caught the attention of American men. The Stetson hat met instant success. Stetson spent a long and profitable life producing a world-famous hat with the Western look. When he died in 1906 his factories were producing two-million hats a year.

Imagine that! A great industry and personal fortune resulted from the suffering of a frail youth. His banishment became his blessing as events unfolded. Had he been healthy, history would have read differently. John B. Stetson's illness had a purpose and was part of a greater plan.

The disciples of Jesus noticed a man blind from birth. They wondered who sinned—this man or his parents, that he was born blind? Their only interest was in finding fault and delivering the proper burden of blame on the right doorstep.

Our Lord countered that the blindness was not the result of sin but that the works of God might be made manifest in him. That man was a miracle just waiting to be performed for God's glory. He was an important part of God's plan (John 9:1-5).

How difficult for us when afflicted, sick, or at wit's end to realize: "This bad situation can become something good through God. In His holy plan for my life, even this has purpose. Nothing can happen to me that God cannot use according to His greater plan."

When Paul's plans for world evangelization were blocked by a Roman imprisonment, he pondered the possibilities. Then he wrote to the Philippians explaining his confidence that God had a master plan which surely included his jailing.

> I want you to know, brethren, that what has happened to me has really served to advance the gospel, so that it has become known throughout the whole praetorian guard and to all the rest that my imprisonment is for Christ, and most of the brethren have been made confident in the Lord because of my imprisonment, and are much more bold to speak the word of God without fear (Phil. 1:12-14).

The Last Word

Dionysius Lardner enjoyed fame. Although his name today sounds more like some character straight out of the comic strips, Lardner was once considered a stable and serious voice in science. When this professor at the prestigious University College in London spoke, people all over the world listened. In the 1830s his outspoken opinions were considered established fact in science and astronomy.

Everyone assumed the good professor's place in history was secure, but Dr. Lardner got caught like others of his era in the trap of narrow thinking. So many of his basic beliefs were proven wrong that embarrassed scientists of today have dismissed him as a crank. Ironically, the world's leading authority then is remembered today only for his absurd predictions.

Steam power brought dramatic changes, including speedy travel by rail. Lardner worried about the effects of high speeds upon frail human bodies. He solemnly warned that passengers traveling near one-hundred miles per hour would lose their breath and die!

Steamships began regular routes on short trips across the English channel. Daring men dreamed of crossing the Atlantic by steam power, but the professor calculated that such a long voyage would require more coal than the ship could ever carry. Reasonable men then dismissed the idea. Yet within six years the steamship *Great Western,* with its improved engine, proved the learned doctor wrong again.

Strange, isn't it? Scientific theories are so often and so easily proven wrong. Precise measurements and statistics do not always lead to the same conclusion.

Lawyers and judges know that expert opinions can be bought to prove almost any point. Pay your money and take your choice in science, medicine, or other technical fields.

Not that the experts can settle the disputed issues. Their usual purpose is provoking doubts about key evidence or challenging the expert testimony presented by the opposing side. Common sense is often sacrificed when evidence that previously appeared conclusive is eventually rejected on the basis of farfetched questions raised by sharp lawyers assisted by scientific testimony.

Shades of Dionysius Lardner! Any expert with the latest word can always prove the earlier expert wrong. Scientists keep changing their minds. They've been wrong before when delivering the latest word. God gave us the first word, and we can trust Him for the last word.

In the beginning God created the heavens and the earth (Gen. 1:1).

Know that the Lord is God! It is he that made us, and we are his (Ps. 100:3).

For we are his workmanship, created in Christ Jesus for good works, which God prepared beforehand, that we should walk in them (Eph. 2:10).

Determination

Not so long ago even the most brilliant astronomers and navigators were still getting lost. Without modern instruments for accurate calculations, they were forced to depend upon unreliable charts and tables. The United States Treasury and a growing insurance industry had similar problems. They needed complicated actuaries and daily interest charts.

Nobody trusted the error-filled books and charts of their day. Would some person please step forward and give a lifetime to this project?

General W. W. Duffield was qualified. As chief of the Coast and Geodetic Survey, he was aware of the great need and determined to help. For twenty-five years he labored on ten-place logarithms, exhaustive tables, and equations. He checked and double-checked his figures for accuracy.

Finally his notes grew into a thick manuscript nearly ready for publication. The scientist carried them in an old-fashioned carpetbag and never let them out of his sight.

That obvious caution, however, must have attracted the attention of a thief who suspected a more spendable fortune. The bag was stolen!

A lifetime of work disappeared. Lesser men would have given

up, but not the general. He started over, certain that the monumental task could be finished sooner the second time than the first.

Years later he completed the eight-hundred-page volume which was published by our government to become a standard reference used daily by thousands in many countries. Duffield's accuracy was rendered obsolete only by our computers of recent years.

Call it determination or just stubbornness, but the world is richer for those who stick to a job they believe important. Too many give up too soon.

What about you? Thinking about quitting? Perhaps the tasks given to you by God aren't as easy as before. Everyone gets weary and discouraged at times. Fatigue is one sign of faithfulness.

Paul counseled the Galatians to hold firm in faith with him. "And let us not grow weary in well-doing, for in due season we shall reap, if we do not lose heart" (Gal. 6:9).

God guarantees a harvest but not on our timetable. We labor in His seasons. He determines when we reap and how successful will be the gain. Our responsibility is to keep busy and to be found faithful.

"Therefore, my beloved brethren, be steadfast, immovable, always abounding in the work of the Lord, knowing that in the Lord your labor is not in vain" (1 Cor. 15:58).

Affliction

To be confined in bed is the ultimate affliction for most people. We prefer active involvement over enforced idleness.

Robert Louis Stevenson languished most of his brief life in bed while wracked with coughing spells caused by tuberculosis. He could have just rolled over and died, but he believed in better things than affliction.

How could he be creative between fitful coughs? The sickly Stevenson turned his imagination loose and dreamed of exciting adventures. He realized that youth all over the world shared his enthusiasm for adventure. Although unhindered by health, most were restricted by tender age or the rough problem of poverty. Since he could still write in bed, why not provide adventure through books? Soon thrilling stories like *Kidnapped* entertained youth and adults alike.

One night his subconscious mind twisted and distorted the real-life details about a criminal described in the newspaper. It was a frightening nightmare which caused the gentle soul to cry in the darkness. Then he woke up in a cold sweat, grateful to be alive in his own bed. Rather than suppress the memory, Stevenson used the dream as his plot for *Dr. Jekyll and Mr. Hyde.*

Life can be like that. What we first consider an unfair blow later turns into an undeserved blessing. Sickness led Stevenson to success. He learned to make profit from pitfall.

We seldom have a choice of circumstances. What we can do is respond to the afflictions which challenge us. We don't give up in life. We give in to God.

> More than that, we rejoice in our sufferings, knowing that suffering produces endurance, and endurance produces character, and character produces hope, and hope does not disappoint us, because God's love has been poured into our hearts through the Holy Spirit which has been given to us (Rom. 5:3-5).

Faith and Works

Twins Chang and Eng made a perfect partnership. They could run, swim, work, and even fight together in tandem against the neighborhood bullies. These brothers were inseparable—literally.

History remembers them as the original Siamese twins, joined physically by a five-inch band from breast to breast. Their shoulders were thus always set toward one another when they walked in a well-coordinated lockstep.

The twins were discovered by an American trader who promised them fame and fortune. They swallowed their pride, became sideshow freaks, and made enough to settle down as gentlemen farmers in North Carolina. They owned slaves, practiced scientific farming methods, and gained more respect than most foreigners.

Soon they were courting sisters who agreed to marriage. Chang and Eng married, built separate homes, and alternated a week with each wife. It was an unusual arrangement but was sanctioned by local clergy. Both unions produced many children.

At age sixty-three Chang's health failed, while Eng was still robust. Their doctors agreed that a surgical separation was possible at the death of either. Then Chang died suddenly in 1874.

A horrified Eng could only moan, "And now I must die also." Within hours he, too, was dead before their doctors could arrive. They had lived and died together.

Autopsies disclosed that while the first died of heart failure, the second suffered from no fatal disease. He had died of sheer fright at being separated from his lifelong union with a brother.

Some things in life ought always to stay together. Faith and works combine in religion to make a perfect partnership which suffers terribly if separated. Faith is the inward soul while works provides the outward body. Faith springs from the heart but is expressed with the hands. Faith comes first.

Good deeds done apart from a heart of faith resemble counterfeit money. Some temporary good might be accomplished along the way, but it won't last. Someone gets hurt down the line holding a worthless bill which must be destroyed. So true works must wait to be authorized or issued by faith.

Faith which is never expressed in loving deed raises doubts while good works confirm sincerity.

> Maintain good conduct among the Gentiles, so that in case they speak against you as wrongdoers, they may see your good deeds and glorify God in the day of visitation (1 Pet. 2:12).
>
> So faith by itself, if it has no works, is dead. For as the body apart from the spirit is dead, so faith apart from works is dead (Jas. 2:17, 26).

Self-Interest

In many ways Mary Mallon was a pleasant person and an asset to a society moving into the twentieth century. Although the skilled cook drifted from job to job, she consistently found work in New York City's finest restaurants.

By curious coincidence, Mary left each job about the time that her customers invariably contracted typhoid! The city's new Department of Health sent an inspector who tracked her down. Mary refused to cooperate, but they eventually made her submit to a physical examination.

The robust lady, seldom sick, turned out to be a rare individual. Her intestinal system was so heavily infested with typhoid bacteria that doctors called her a human culture tube. While personally immune, she was a carrier of that fatal disease.

The public feared "Typhoid Mary" and made her *persona non grata* everywhere. Since health authorities had no legal power to prevent her employment around food, however, Mary just changed her identity and took new jobs.

Thus began five years of cloak-and-dagger efforts by authorities to shadow the elusive Mary. Where typhoid struck, they found Mary and warned her latest employer who promptly fired her. Finally, laws were passed to protect the public. Mary was confined to a hospital and closely watched for the rest of her life.

Tragic, you think? How could anyone be so callous to spread disease and death just because she enjoyed cooking? Self-interest can be so blind and thoughtless. How true the proverb, "Every way of a man is right in his own eyes" (Prov. 21:2).

Two boys in Dallas were warned on an Independence Day about fireworks. They should stop shooting rockets because wood shingles might ignite in that hot, dry weather. The boys ignored the danger. After all, they were having fun. Three neighbors lost their homes that day in the fire which followed.

Then what about the host who has no problems "handling his liquor"? He throws a party and pours drinks for all. The pressure is subtle but sure on those who try to resist. Be sociable, have a drink, and have fun.

Perhaps the host makes sure every drunk guest gets home safely. But that is only part of his responsibility. How can he care for those who become addicted to alcoholic beverages? One in every ten persons who drinks socially later becomes addicted. Statistically, that is a higher proportion than those infected by "Typhoid Mary's" food!

Laws could help control some abuses and dangers caused by those who think only of themselves. But a better approach is God's love in action.

Love is patient and kind; love is not jealous or boastful; it is not arrogant or rude. Love does not insist on its own way (1 Cor. 13:4-5).

Do nothing from selfishness or conceit, but in humility count others better than yourselves. Let each of you look not only to his own interests, but also to the interests of others (Phil. 2:3-4).

A Missouri Miracle

The fire chief shook his head sadly. "All we can do is slow down the fire, but we can't stop it. The attic is gone while the second floor is engulfed in smoke. Best let the neighbors keep moving everything out of this ground level."

Thus it was settled. This aging mansion, long a local landmark in the farming community of Advance, Missouri, was burning to the ground. Lyman and Thomza Zimmerman would be homeless that night.

All morning long the volunteer firemen pumped water to buy time for neighbors and friends who organized a moving miracle. Professionals in the transfer industry could not have done more with a month's notice.

Antiques were carried outside, packed in cartons which mysteriously appeared, and loaded in a procession of pickups. They stripped the lower floor of everything not bolted or built-in. Even a priceless chandelier survived without a scratch.

Word spread. From thirty miles away a television news team raced to catch the action. As the flames consumed their beloved home and friends completed the rescue effort, color cameras recorded a poignant interview.

The Zimmermans were shocked and sad, but not bitter. They

lost their home but not their faith. Listen to the testimony of this older, childless couple.

Thomza: "Yes, we lost half of our lifetime possessions. But we saved the other half. At our age, that's enough."

Lyman: "This is beautiful. When a man sees how many friends he really has, he learns to count his true blessings. It may be worth it all!"

The Zimmermans surveyed the ruins and praised God. They were alive. Their remaining possessions were safely stored. Friends had even moved a mobile camper to the scene where they could live.

How exciting that God offered some unnoticed blessings. An unusual wind had blown the heat away from their favorite shade trees which survived. Within a few weeks spring arrived to the sound of crickets and carpenters.

The Zimmermans camped through summer while a lovely home rose on the same spot. From a new kitchen window Thomza soon enjoyed the familiar songbirds again.

It could have been different. Some people lead such isolated and independent lives that friends are too few for help in crises.

Others hold too tightly to earthly possessions and suffer permanent shock at such losses. They forget what they saved and focus on what they lost.

Still others blame God while failing to recognize His hand in adversity. When that happens, let the discouraged journey to the "Show-Me State" where they can sit under shade of the Zimmerman trees and listen to a Missouri miracle that belongs to all mankind. "We know that in everything God works for good with those who love him" (Rom. 8:28).

Our Advocate

Some things are handled best by others. Physicians say that the doctor who treats himself has a fool for a patient.

Lawyers understood this tricky truth. The smartest attorneys seek help when they are personally summoned into court to defend themselves.

And now a twenty-five-year-old Tulsa, Oklahoma, man agrees. Marshall George Cummings, Jr. first believed that he could do better than any lawyer in defending himself on a purse-snatching charge.

The cocky con man chose to personally cross-examine his victim who was testifying against him in court. He should have left the questioning to a real lawyer.

Trying to make a dramatic point, Cummings asked: "Did you get a good look at my face when I took your purse?"

The damage was done. His slip served the same as a confession. Although Cummings then decided to accept a public defender, it was too late. He was convicted and sentenced to ten years in prison!

While few of us expect to stand trial on those charges, the Bible declares that we are guilty of sin. Jesus warned us about a judgment which is coming.

> When the Son of man comes in his glory, and all the angels with him, then he will sit on his glorious throne. Before him will be gathered all the nations, and he will separate them one from another as a shepherd separates the sheep from the goats (Matt. 25:31-32).

No hesitation here. It's heaven for some and hell for the rest.

Then he will say to those at his left hand, "Depart from me, you cursed, into the eternal fire prepared for the devil and his angels." And they will go away into eternal punishment, but the righteous into eternal life (Matt. 25:41, 46)

In that day of final reckoning, Jesus is both Judge and jury. "The Father judges no one, but has given all judgment to the Son, that all may honor the Son, even as they honor the Father" (John 5:22-23).

Look again. Jesus also serves as prosecutor and chief witness against the guilty! In that final scene as human history is reviewed and individuals throughout all the ages are judged, the angels stand by as heavenly observers. Jesus will not dishonor the faithful by disregarding justice. "But he who denies me before men will be denied before the angels of God" (Luke 12:9).

But we who are redeemed and trust our souls into the care of Jesus will not be disappointed. Although we Christians must appear before God in a judgment of works, we are to be released or excused from that dreaded final judgment. (See Matt. 16:27; Rom. 2:6; 14:12; 2 Cor. 5:10 for references concerning the judgment of works for a Christian.) We shall look with relief to see Jesus waiting for us with open arms. He has decided to become our Defender, our Advocate before God. "But if any one does sin, we have an advocate with the Father, Jesus Christ the righteous; and he is the expiation for our sins" (1 John 2:1-2).

We have no need to defend ourselves in that day. Best leave our concerns with Jesus. He is able to represent us. "And I tell you, every one who acknowledges me before men, the Son of man also will acknowledge before the angels of God" (Luke 12:8).

Perfect Sight

On a clear day American spy satellites orbiting twenty miles high routinely transmit sharp pictures of objects the size of golf balls on the Russian ground below. For most of us that kind of sophisticated technology is almost unbelievable, but our own eyes can be just as amazing.

Take the eyesight of Joseph P. Stevens, for example. While cruising down a Rhode Island stretch of I-195 near Providence, he spotted his own auto being hauled on the back of a flatbed truck. One glance was enough. It was definitely his car which had been stolen earlier.

What's so remarkable about that sighting? Just this. His 1971 Ford Torino was no longer a full-sized compact. Now it was crushed into a 6-inch tall, 18-foot long slab of metal and loaded on the bottom of twenty other cars—a real compact!

How was he so sure? He recognized a bumper sticker and a rag waving from what was once the car's trunk.

After unsuccessfully trying to force the truck driver to pull over, Stevens followed the cargo to a truck stop where he telephoned police. Sure enough. Identification numbers proved it was his car. The crushed remains were confiscated by authorities and an investigation began. One detective, still marveling at the keen eyes of Stevens, suggested the man ought to get a medal. Stevens would have settled for his car.

The truth is plain to see. Most of us have sharp eyes when claiming what belongs to us. Even more, we easily recognize our loved ones at great distance as the loving father did while waiting for his prodigal son.

And why not? God must have carefully planned for our hearts and minds to aid in sight. What we lack in comparison to spy satellites, we make up with emotion. Thus we are much like our Maker who sees all from His heavenly throne.

The Bible overflows with many illustrations of God's eyes focused upon us. Hanani, speaking as a prophet sent to King Asa of Judah, condemned the monarch for relying upon a Syrian ally instead of trusting the Lord who sees all. "For the eyes of the Lord run to and fro throughout the whole earth, to show his might in behalf of those whose heart is blameless toward him" (2 Chron. 16:9).

The psalmist declared, "Behold, the eye of the Lord is on those who fear him, on those who hope in his steadfast love. The eyes of the Lord are toward the righteous" (Ps. 33:18; 34:15).

We can never lose ourselves out of God's sight—not even on purpose. After Adam and Eve sinned by disobeying God to sample the forbidden fruit, they felt guilty. Like children they tried to hide themselves in the garden from God. Don't be misled by God calling to the man, "Where are you?" The all-seeing Creator knew exactly where they were. But He wanted Adam and Eve to see themselves, to find themselves. His question was meant to provoke thought, not to gain information. "He who formed the eye, does he not see?" (Ps. 94:9).

Here is the conclusion. God knows our every move not just because He has sharp eyes. It's a matter of possession. We belong to Him and will never be out of His perfect sight. And that's the most incredible but comforting fact of all.

Break a Leg

When Bob Kirk slipped on ice, he got the biggest break in a most inventive career. His good fortune began after the doctor discovered an injured leg was fractured in three places and needed a heavy cast.

Nobody looks forward to that kind of problem, but the Chicago inventor was determined to make the best of a bad situation. After twenty-five years of creative thought leading to only minor inventions, Kirk wasn't ready to quit. Someday inspiration would strike for a major money-maker. At least now he would have some extra time to think and plan.

In this case inspiration painfully struck weeks later when the cast was being removed. The doctor's cast cutter penetrated below the hard plaster into sensitive skin. Ouch! Someone ought to invent a safety guard for this electric saw. Kirk did just that.

The Stryker Corporation was so delighted with his little invention that it offered generous royalties plus an annual retainer for further advice. The manufacturer knew nearly four-hundred-thousand owners of the cast cutters and believed 80 percent of them were hot prospects for purchase of this safety device which is so easily attached.

The broken leg is healed now, but these days the fifty-four-year-old former boxer and coach can laugh about his route to success. It goes to prove that a positive attitude finds blessings in any problem.

Now what about your broken plans or shattered dreams? Don't give up. Somehow you must turn these bad breaks into blessings for better life, so seek God for some out-of-this-world help. The

Great Physician who heals broken bones can mend even broken hearts. He waits patiently to help when we stumble. God listens for our prayers as we reach the end of our rope or cry in despair and discouragement.

No matter how bad the situation, God can make something good come from it. Even if "he maketh me to lie down" in the bed of affliction or illness, victory can still be mine. I don't have to give up when too weak to get up. I look up and seek God's blessing from that buffeting.

For years Henry Wadsworth Longfellow suffered from insomnia. Though his body needed rest, his mind refused to accept a normal night of refreshing sleep. How could the poet get rest enough to be creative the next day?

In desperation, Longfellow decided he would not wait for a tuckered-out tomorrow to write. If he could not sleep, he would light a lamp and compose his thoughts while still under the covers. During a long and creative career Longfellow insisted that his best poetry and verse resulted from those sleepless nights.

The principle is clear. We aren't expected to take every defeat or discouragement lying down. We Christians have the ultimate resource of a God who helps us turn defeat into victory. "But thanks be to God, who in Christ always leads us in triumph, and through us spreads the fragrance of the knowledge of him everywhere" (2 Cor. 2:14).

The Choice

After loading a month's supplies on the wagon, a farmer and his wife called for their daughter who had remained inside in the general store. She stood before a counter in front of a colorful selection of hard candies.

The storekeeper complimented the little girl for being so good while her folks were busy. Would she like to reach into a candy jar for a free handful? The little girl smiled but hesitated, so the owner finally reached into the jar himself and gave her a generous handful.

On the way home her parents asked: "Why didn't you reach into the jar? You are not that shy." With that same delightful smile, she replied: "Because his hands were bigger!"

Thomas Edison would have appreciated her wisdom. In 1870 the twenty-three-year-old inventor arrived in New York from Boston. His head was full of ideas for great inventions, but his pockets were empty.

Because Edison had worked earlier as a telegraph operator, he headed for a Western Union office. Did the manager need an inventor? No, but he did have some equipment which his repairmen were unable to fix.

Edison restored the equipment and hung around as an unsalaried troubleshooter. General Marshall Lefferts, head of the company, took an interest in him and promised to "settle up" soon.

After the youthful genius made a dramatic improvement in stock tickers which often "ran wild," Leffert decided Edison deserved a reward for his many projects. "Well, young man, how much do you think they are worth?"

Edison figured a thousand dollars would be fine and two thousand would be fair. He thought about asking for five thousand. Or should he settle for three?

Edison was indeed handy with his hands, but he was inexperienced in finance. Unsure of himself, he decided to trust Lefferts who was known as an honest man. "General, suppose you make me an offer."

Leffert responded, "How would forty-thousand dollars strike you?" The young inventor turned pale and barely managed to mumble his approval.

He learned a valuable lesson that day. Leffert's generosity had been greater than Edison's greed. The inventor invested his bonanza toward a research shop in which he later made multiple millions of dollars from other inventions.

Have you learned the same lesson about God? He can be trusted to give us better than what we might choose on our own. Unfortunately, some people are always demanding special favors from Him. Unable to patiently await His blessings, they scheme for what they want. But God always saves the best in life for those who leave the choices to Him. After all, His hands are bigger!

"He who did not spare his own Son but gave him up for us all, will he not also give us all things with him?" (Rom. 8:32).

Change

Ever wonder why the Russian peasants so eagerly joined the Bolshevik Revolution in 1918? Historians say the nation was hopelessly corrupt in monarchy, government, and even the church. Society had stagnated so much that people were ready for a change—any change.

Before revolution erupted in that moribund state, the Russian czar once noticed a sentry guarding a small patch of weeds. How strange. When he asked the reason for such an unusual assignment, the sentry shrugged, "Just obeying orders."

The commanding officer was asked who gave this absurd order. The sentry didn't know. It was just part of his command—something that had always been done as long as anyone could remember.

Intrigued, the czar ordered the archives to be searched page by page. Finally the mystery was solved. Long ago Catherine the

Great had planted a rose bush on that spot and ordered a guard to protect it from careless feet.

Eventually the bush died, but no one dared cancel the order. Then Catherine died. Years passed and the order was never changed. Tradition ruled long after everyone had forgotten the original purpose.

No matter what the organization, some changes are necessary in the course of time. Otherwise, we will suffer like the Russians. They wasted twenty-four hours a day for a hundred years guarding a patch of weeds!

Even churches must change as time moves on—new ministries, different directions, various emphases. Otherwise, the seven last words of a dead church are heard again: "We never did it that way before!"

Methods change—but never the message about an unchanging Christ who died for us, was buried, and raised again the third day. "Jesus Christ is the same yesterday and today and for ever" (Heb. 13:8).

Memberships change, but never the joy of our fellowship. Rural congregations sometimes welcome the new folks so warmly that the little brown church in the vale grows and grows to become a bustling, suburban giant. Or perhaps it is a blue-collar church located in a neighborhood overwhelmed by an ethnic invasion. In a brief time the old church declines, but then it blossoms as members minister to their new neighbors who replenish the ranks.

Of all the changes in churches, the most basic and common is that change called conversion. This is the starting place, a radical rebirth of old sinners into new creatures of the spirit. Only a regenerated membership is accepted by Christ.

"Therefore, if any one is in Christ, he is a new creation; the old has passed away, behold, the new has come" (2 Cor. 5:17).

Nothing New?

Back in 1843 the first United States Patent Commissioner, Henry Ellsworth, felt "the advancement of the arts taxes our credulity and seems to presage that period when human improvement must end."

Did he really mean that? Could he have actually believed that there wasn't much left to invent, change, or improve in this old world? No wonder Ellsworth didn't last long on that job.

Nowdays the head of this government agency must be the most open-minded person in the world. It is a basic requirement for the job where technological and medical miracles developed in secret make their first public appearance. As recently as fifty years ago no one in their right mind could have envisioned our basic electronic gadgets like calculators and computers commonly used by children. Yes, the patent people have to take some crazy ideas very seriously.

Of course, the vast majority of these requests for patent protection are not original ideas. Some inventions touted as revolutionary turn out to be the same old mousetrap painted a different color. Others are clearly impossible procedures represented only by indecipherable scribbles on grocery sacks.

Yet someone has to impartially investigate each request for a patient. An official ruling must be issued in a gentle but not gullible spirit. That is the commissioner's job which makes him a busy man. Exploding technology and creative inventors are producing nearly one-hundred-thousand patents per year. For every patent granted there are dozens of preliminary inquiries and requests that didn't succeed.

Can you imagine a man in this position acting like many bored folks do? You know the attitude: "So what? I've seen it all. There's nothing new for me!"

One thing for certain. There is nothing new about that attitude. Centuries ago a bored king, destined to become the wisest of the ancients, lamented: "There is nothing new under the sun" (Eccl. 1:9). Fortunately for Solomon, his search for the meaning of life ended in God and produced a happier philosophy with a positive outlook.

We have it easier. The *New* Testament—there is that word again—teaches that the God of old came in Jesus to make all things new. When we give ourselves to Him, our old lives die and are replaced by the new. "Therefore, if any one is in Christ, he is a new creation; the old has passed away, behold the new has come" (2 Cor. 5:17).

There you have it. The patent office isn't the only place where many things new under the sun gather. In the kingdom of God we are made new under the Son.

Perseverance

Does anyone remember Enrico Caruso? His polished and professional voice once provided the most admired music in the world. In his day no one was more famous than the consistent Caruso who paid the price in perseverance before he ever succeeded.

How easily the world forgets that Caruso was never born a singer. Early in his life he labored at a menial factory job for twelve years. Exhaustion and discouragement could not stop him from studying and practicing every night. Caruso felt confident that his diligence in preparation would bring rich rewards. He never turned back.

When an opportunity for stardom finally arrived, he walked onto the stage confident. Then butterflies in the tummy caused his voice to crack. People laughed, so he fled the theater in tears. But next day he resumed his regular practice.

When Caruso received a second chance to fill in for an ill tenor, the audience hissed him. No matter. Perseverance paid off. He kept trying until he succeeded. Those early years of adversity taught him far more than easy fame.

Do you have that kind of perseverance that endures even when rewards seem questionable? Faith demands discipline. We must set our sights on the long run with confidence that the higher path is the best route. Shortcuts are not allowed.

As a construction superintendent approached retirement, he pondered the uncertain rewards of his honest career. What had he gained? Others had turned their heads and accepted bribes, but he had resisted those temptations. Soon his employer would give him a nice watch, say some kind words, and promptly forget his faithfulness.

Bitterness slowly and silently crept into his heart. On the last project under his administration, a beautiful house, the employee decided it was time to feather his own nest as he supervised the construction of the lovely house. For some reason his boss seemed preoccupied and left most of the purchasing and decorating details in the superintendent's hands. "Just do as if it were your own," the employer said. So he took advantage of the opportunity by substituting cheap materials and pocketing the difference. He cut corners, building a shoddy structure for some rich stranger who probably didn't deserve it anyway.

The project was completed the same day he officially retired. But instead of the customary watch, the boss explained that his most trusted employee would receive something better—this last house. It had been planned all along as a surprise retirement gift from a grateful employer. The superintendent swallowed hard as the terrible truth dawned upon him. If only he had kept faithful. He had quit too soon to reap the rewards of honesty. In trying to cheat someone else, he succeeded in cheating himself.

All good comes to those who wait in patience and work in earnest. Perseverance plays a key role in that spiritual quality of faith which keeps a hand to the plow. Too many quit too soon. They know *what* is right, but they forget *when* is right. God remains in charge of when success or rewards arrive. "And let us not grow weary in well-doing, for in due season we shall reap, if we do not lose heart" (Gal. 6:9).

Payday Someday

Daniel Webster believed in an honest day's labor for an honest day's pay. But what if a prospective client could not afford to pay for that day of honest work?

The young attorney also believed that in life most accounts usually balance out for generous givers. For that reason he never took shortcuts even in time-consuming cases of charity.

A depressed citizen sought his services in a complicated case involving an insurance matter. The poor man deserved justice, but his twenty dollars in life savings was too small an amount to interest other lawyers. So he begged the inexperienced Webster to represent him.

Webster took the case and journeyed to Boston where he consulted a law library. After much study he found a legal precedent which won the case easily. Unfortunately, the twenty-dollar fee did not even cover his basic expenses of travel and lodging.

The Christian attorney was not discouraged. Someday every good deed will be repaid in full. He had confidence that with God in control of the Christian reward system, it would be payday someday.

That kind of dedication and character brought fame to the able attorney. Prosperity followed. Webster forgot about the costly good deed.

Then years later an affluent family asked his help. Their lawyer was ill. Would Webster substitute for them at court tomorrow? It was already late in the day. Webster tactfully declined, explaining the impossibility of preparing a legal position on such short notice.

The people persisted. Money was no object. Wouldn't he just take a quick look at their papers? Finally Webster consented, but only to look. Then he smiled and agreed to take the case which he won the next day with ease.

How? He recognized the same issue as his old twenty-dollar case. The handsome fee more than compensated his previous loss. It was payday that day!

Learn the lesson of every good farmer who gives his best grain to the prepared soil. In due time he reaps bountiful rewards. "The point is this: he who sows sparingly will also reap sparingly, and he who sows bountifully will also reap bountifully" (2 Cor. 9:6).

Refuse to be selfish with your acts of kindness. Invest in the kingdom of God through your local church, but give yourself also in good deeds for others. God pays wonderful dividends. "Give, and it will be given to you. . . . For the measure you give will be the measure you get back (Luke 6:38).

Escape

A daring but careless lad lost his footing while climbing on a roof of an abandoned building. He slipped and tumbled off the roof of the three-story structure. Seeing the ground rush forward to greet him, he cried out in panic: "God, save me!"

Just then the fall was stopped by a rusty nail which caught his belt. He hung there for a moment, wiped his brow and looked up into the sky. "Never mind now, God. I done saved myself with this old nail."

What kind of theology is that? Call it *me-ology*. We who are self-centered by human nature need not study to master this human-based philosophy. We learn it naturally.

We get into trouble and pray desperately for a miracle. Then somehow things settle down without doom, disaster, or death. We are released from our worst fears and promptly forget we ever called upon God.

Give the boy credit for one point. Although blind to God's answered prayer via a rusty nail, and brash enough to take credit for delivering himself, at least he did not put God on hold. He went back to God and canceled his urgent request.

Some frantically call on God and then leave Him waiting on the line without so much as "thanks" or "good-bye." Even common telephone courtesy requires us to finish the conversation and sign off.

But a better way is recognizing how God does indeed respond to our needs. He watches over us and keeps us safe day after day. In this providential care, sudden and dramatic miracles are not always necessary.

Often God answers our prayers without removing the thorn or the painful problem. He has a better way. We demand an easier life, but instead God offers us strength to overcome. We grow stronger and better prepared for the next problem.

The best way to escape great problems and temptations is to let God help you endure the situation. "God is faithful, and he will not let you be tempted beyond your strength, but with the temptation will also provide the way of escape, that you may be able to endure it" (1 Cor. 10:13).

Did you catch that? A route of escape is provided when we learn to bear the burden with God's help. How mysterious are the ways of God! But how practical. The Almighty did not create us as pampered customers of a divine delivery service for miracles on demand. He is eager, however, to assist us in growing stronger for endurance. "I can do all things in him who strengthens me" (Phil. 4:13).

Pray as if your deliverance depends totally upon God. Work as if your deliverance depends totally upon yourself. Then trust God to help you master the crushing burdens, the temptations, and problems of daily life. "And my God will supply every need of yours according to his riches in glory in Christ Jesus" (Phil. 4:19).

Determined

A mighty empire had some rough moments. Rome's greatest enemy was Carthage, led by Hannibal who nearly destroyed the Eternal City before the major Roman era got underway.

In his dramatic invasion of Roman territory, this creative Carthaginian ignored the heavily defended southern coast. Rome's northern border, protected by the snow-covered Alps, was unguarded because it had never been crossed by an army. "Impossible," they said.

In a stroke of military genius, Hannibal used elephants to accomplish the impossible. Those great beasts ferried supplies over the mountains as freezing troops scaled the frozen heights. But their greatest impact came in battle. The surprised defenders fled in fear before these ancient armored tanks which charged their ranks.

For the next eighteen months Hannibal destroyed every army

the Romans hastily threw before him. Rome lost sixty-thousand men in an unprecedented series of disasters.

Nothing could stop the Carthaginians. Many military experts consider Hannibal's maneuvers and strategy the most brilliant in history. In the summer of 216 BC he camped only three miles outside the capital city walls.

Others would have recognized the inevitable and sued for peace, but not the Romans. Theirs was a will to win. Even if Rome fell, they knew Carthage could not send enough soldiers to occupy their land. They would fight on to death. They stood united.

Rather than recriminations, the senate commended the defeated General Varro "because he had not despaired of the Commonwealth." The very land on which Hannibal's army was encamped came up for sale and brought its full market value!

Against such spirit not even Hannibal's military genius could prevail. He won every battle but not the war. His victories cost him so dearly that he could not afford to win again. He had run out of troops.

That summer Hannibal gave up and fled. The Romans had discovered the key to victory—total commitment unto death. Their next step to world dominion came easily.

Early Christians shared that same spirit of determined commitment unto death. Like Hannibal, believers in Christ invaded every land with good news about Jesus who died and lives evermore. But more like the Romans, these Christians displayed a willingness to die. Death could not defeat them. Martyrs multiplied into multitudes. The blood of these martyrs became the seed of the church, as one ancient historian marveled.

How could Christians be so determined even in the face of death? They had the greatest example of all. Jesus died willingly and then was raised to life. In one of His last messages this risen Christ had reminded His disciples: "Be faithful unto death, and I will give you the crown of life" (Rev. 2:10).

Wisdom

In brains and brilliance, few people equal a fast learner named Jay Luo. After less than three years in grade school, Jay skipped high school going straight into college. Only thirty months later he graduated from Boise (Idaho) State University with honors. All that by age twelve!

Just how smart is the pint-sized scholar and youngest college graduate in America? On the basis of book learning and test taking, Jay's intelligence quotient (I.Q.) ranks on the level of genius. That's really smart.

On the other hand, "smartness" is not all important. Plodders with ordinary minds have a habit of succeeding in life where genius fails. There must be something beyond basic intellect which man-made measurements just cannot gauge.

As a child Thomas Edison was anything but brilliant. One teacher described him as "addled." In truth, Edison was a systematic thinker who seldom invented by luck or flashes of inspired genius. His curiosity, practicality, mechanical nature, and open mind made him an ideal researcher. But his best habit was hard work.

Edison believed that success depends upon 1 percent inspiration and 99 percent perspiration. That's why in his stubborn search for a light bulb filament, he persisted after a thousand experiments failed.

A smarter man might have given up, but Edison looked on the bright side. He had now discovered a thousand ways that would not work. He was getting closer!

Not that Edison was really "addled" or even a slow thinker.

Perhaps we push the point too far that brilliance is not required for success, but we can never overemphasize what old-timers used to describe as "common sense sanctified by the Holy Spirit." This ability beyond brains is best summarized in the biblical concept of wisdom.

Unlike pure genius or native intelligence, wisdom can be developed by seeking after God and living according to His standards. We are even commanded to seek this blessing. "So teach us to number our days that we may get a heart of wisdom" (Ps. 90:12).

Solomon sought a heart of wisdom. Before being crowned king, he was approached by God in a dream. "And God said, 'Ask what I shall give you' " (1 Kings 3:5).

Solomon responded: "Give thy servant therefore an understanding mind to govern thy people, that I may discern between good and evil" (v. 9).

The request met with God's favor. "Because you have asked this, and have not asked for yourself long life or riches or the life of your enemies, but have asked for your understanding to discern what is right, behold, I now do according to your word. Behold, I give you a wise and discerning mind" (vv. 11-12).

Next in the narrative comes history's most famous example of wisdom. Two harlots shared a house together, and each gave birth to a child. After one infant died, both women came to the king claiming the surviving child. How could the wise king be certain which was the real mother? Solomon ordered a sword be brought into his presence. The infant would be divided so each woman would receive half a baby!

One woman was horrified. This should never happen, so she quickly agreed to give up her claim so that the baby might live. But the other woman had shown no similar concern. If she could not have all of a living baby, then half a baby would do. That way both babies would be dead and both mothers equal.

At this point everyone recognized the rightful mother. She

received her child alive, but it was Solomon's wisdom which set the stage for such a clear judgment.

Many centuries later an American President demonstrated similar examples of wit and wisdom. Historians generally concede that Abraham Lincoln was not among our brightest Presidents. In his famous debates with Stephen F. Douglas, the rough log splitter was bested in finer points of logic. Douglas thought fast on his feet and demonstrated a commanding grasp of details and knowledge about many subjects. His eloquence and oratory awed the crowds.

Lincoln lost the debates and the senate seat he sought. Yet Lincoln was no loser in character, morals, and other godly virtues which comprise wisdom. His spiritual sensitivity, homespun wit, and honest heart proved better than raw intellect. When the people needed a president for troubled times, they chose the wisdom of Lincoln over the brilliance of Douglas.

Wisdom is more than an earthly characteristic. The Bible links wisdom with those who follow God and seek His will. We need not be geniuses to know that getting along with God helps us get along with our fellowmen on earth.

"The fear of the Lord is the beginning of wisdom; a good understanding have all those who practice it" (Ps. 111:10).

Failure

In 1893 Thomas Edison designed a little machine he called a kinetoscope. Always a businessman alert for inventions leading to profit, Edison equipped this device with a coin slot. For a nickel the viewer could see moving pictures inside much better than those of a penny arcade.

So Edison invested his money, but the venture failed in the marketplace. Edison confessed: "I am very doubtful there is any commercial future in it." Had anyone offered a few dollars for those manufacturing rights, it would have probably been a quick sale.

Lucky Edison. One day he opened the box and focused a picture on the wall. That fascinated him. Instead of paying money to look into a box, perhaps people would buy an admission ticket to see the same sight on a wall. So Edison removed the coin slot, and within a year that same machine was attracting a world of attention. His kinetoscope became the film projector which launched a new industry of motion pictures with entertainment for all America.

Strange, but failure often makes fertile soil for the seeds of success. Call it persistence, patience, or plain luck—but Edison changed the world with an idea that earlier struck out. Failure can be followed by success the second time around!

Many people never get back up after once being knocked down. They become discouraged and give up, complain about bad breaks and a raw deal, or they make excuses. But some succeed at the same task where they earlier stumbled.

When Barnabas and Paul left on their first missionary journey from Antioch, they invited John Mark to assist them. The young man displayed great promise. They counted on him, but at Pamphylia Mark left them. We don't know whether the problem was homesickness, discouragement, or personal problems, but Mark quit and returned home to Jerusalem.

John Mark's failure did not set well with Paul. During preparations for a second journey, Barnabas wanted to give Mark a second chance. Paul objected so strongly that "there arose a sharp contention, so that they separated from each other. Barnabas took Mark with him and sailed away to Cyprus, but Paul chose Silas and departed" (Acts 15:39).

The successful missionary team actually split over the issue of Mark's earlier failure. But Barnabas, bighearted and always the encourager, had his way. Mark got a second chance with him and proved faithful after all.

Years later Paul wrote in his last letter from prison to Timothy: "Get Mark and bring him with you; for he is very useful in serving me" (2 Tim. 4:11).

Failure was followed by success. The same disciple was now viewed in a different light. Mark became useful in serving Paul. How encouraging. As long as we are alive and willing to start over with God, our failures need not be final.

"And I am sure that he who began a good work in you will bring it to completion at the day of Jesus Christ" (Phil. 1:6).

The Past Is Past

Besides having eyes in the back of the head, teachers are also supposed to have a good eye for young talent. They seem to instinctively sense who among their students are destined for success. Or so it seems when Johnny makes good and his teacher is interviewed years later. The quotes always sound the same. "I knew little Johnny had ability. I'm glad to have encouraged him toward success."

But sometimes little Johnny is a late bloomer who doesn't impress his teachers. Consider these high achievers who started out low.

Henry Ward Beecher, perhaps one of America's most gifted preacher-philosophers, was described by a teacher as a poor writer and a miserable speller. She was not the first teacher to misjudge an extremely gifted but bored student. Beecher needed a few years to find himself spiritually. God waited, Beecher responded, and America received the blessings from a talented minister who moved with God.

Louis Pasteur's major professor remembered the great physician-researcher as "the meekest, smallest and least promising student in my class." At least this teacher was honest! But history offers a brighter assessment of the researcher who developed the process of milk preservation that bears his name—pasteurization. The French scientist overcame his past with flying colors.

Napoleon Bonaparte impressed few of his military school instructors where he graduated forty-second in a class of forty-three. After the "little general" proved to be Europe's most brilliant and charismatic commander in history, his teachers all claimed he was much smarter than his low rank. Napoleon never needed to be concerned about his past low grades.

Ulysses S. Grant barely made it through West Point. No one questioned his ability, for the young Grant excelled enough in math to dream of someday teaching at his military school. But Grant lacked determination and discipline. His instructors and later commanders agreed he might hang around in the army as a lowly lieutenant, but little was expected of him.

After ten years Grant left the military under a cloud. Some blamed his habit of strong drink, but in truth the army officer stationed in far-off California missed his bride in Missouri. In a lonely fit of despondency, the young groom simply resigned his commission to return home. Civilian life was no better, as he drifted from failures in business to farming.

Then the Civil War erupted, and Grant returned to his original career. None of his contemporaries from West Point wanted him in their commands, so Grant found an unlikely bunch of Illinois volunteers to lead. From there he rose to lead the entire Union army. He quickly outranked all his former instructors and commanding officers!

The lesson for us? We need not be a prisoner of our past. Anything is possible for the person who uses wisely one's God-given talents. And when that person is a Christian, an added dimension of spiritual power makes an even greater difference.

Look at Simon Peter, the apostle who had a lot to live down. So bold and brave at times, but yet weak and unstable. That was Peter, a man of contrasts who could move on a moment's notice from deeds of courage to acts of cowardice.

While others wrestled with the true identity of Jesus, Peter could grasp that deep, hidden truth. "You are the Christ, the Son of the living God," Peter declared in a flash of inspiration. Jesus commended Peter, "Blessed are you Simon Bar-Jona! For flesh and blood has not revealed this to you, but my Father who is in heaven." Yet in the very next scene this same Peter so strongly resisted the Lord that Jesus looked at him and delivered a stinging rebuke as if he were Satan. "Get behind me, Satan! You are a hindrance to me; for you are not on the side of God, but of men" (Matt. 16:16-17, 23).

Following the sad occasion of the last supper, Jesus cautioned his disciples: "You will all fall away because of me this night." Again Peter protested and tried to correct Jesus. "Though they all fall away because of you, I will never fall away." Would he never learn? Before the night would end, this overly confident and cocky apostle would deny Jesus not once but three times! But until then, Peter wanted to have the last word. "Even if I must die with you, I will not deny you" (Matt. 26:31, 33, 35).

What a past to put behind him! Yet unlike Judas who hung himself in remorse, Simon Peter picked himself up from his frequent failures and finally fulfilled his destiny. After the resurrection Simon became the man he was meant to be—Peter or *Petros,* which in Greek means *the rock.* A nickname given him by the Lord finally came true. The apostle with feet of clay turned into a spiritual rock (Mark 3:16).

Paul reached that point later in life when his past did not matter. Forgiven sins ought to be forgotten sins. They are removed as far from us as the east is from the west. Let us march on. "But one thing I do, forgetting what lies behind and straining forward to what lies ahead, I press on toward the goal for the prize of the upward call of God in Christ Jesus" (Phil. 3:13-14).

Born Loser

Where else but in the comic strips could we meet such a lovable little loser? Make no mistake about it, Charlie Brown is the original born loser, with his trademarks—an oversized head and stubby legs.

He knows humiliation and is rejected on a regular basis by Lucy, Linus, and every other kid on the block. Even his own dog, Snoopy, outshines and outsmarts him.

Ever wonder where creator Charlie Schulz got his inspiration for this eager blockhead whose main talent is failure? He didn't go far to find a real-life loser when he began drawing.

The famous cartoonist offers a frank confession. The public Charlie Brown represents the youthful failures of a private Charlie Schulz. This comic strip is autobiographic.

In the classroom Schulz was a troubled student always behind in his studies. His physically uncoordinated body humiliated him in competitive sports. On the social scene in high school he never once had the courage to ask a girl for a date.

Surely the man who draws the world's most popular comic strip today anticipated during boyhood his future success. Right? Wrong! Schulz seldom dreamed of success because everything he did failed. Even his high school yearbook rejected the cartoons Schulz submitted.

His was not a rapid rise to the top but a slow climb of hard work and daily drudgery. Yet Schulz never gave up, because as a young man he realized that God loved him and had a plan for good things in his life. His religious family and supportive church accepted him as he was and encouraged him to find God's will.

Schulz surrendered his life to the ministry and was willing to preach even though his youthful voice lacked authority. No matter. After several years of searching for a way to serve God, he found his pulpit in the comic strip. Success came finally after that long period of preparation through failure.

Success. Ah, that's a sweet sound to our society today. We love the success stories of men like Charles Schulz. But let us not forget how failure preceded success. Perhaps that is why we so identify with Charlie Brown. He has great intentions and lofty goals but seldom succeeds. He is the bewildered type who wonders, "How can I keep on losing when I'm so sincere?"

Moderation

When Henry M. Stanley was exploring the dense forests of Africa, he encountered his most formidable foe in a tribe of Wambutti dwarfs. Despite their small size and tiny weapons, they feared no one. Their miniature arrows delivered a deadly poison more powerful than an elephant gun.

So what was that strong substance which caused certain death? The primitive tribesmen had learned to make poison from one of nature's best foods—honey.

The Wambutti dwarfs aren't the only people who can take something good and produce bad results. With our great abundance and prosperity, we Americans tend to dig our graves with a fork. Benjamin Franklin, probably our most practical philosopher, correctly advised: "To lengthen thy years, lessen thy meals."

Many drink to excess. A twenty-nine-year-old woman was warned repeatedly that she might drink herself to death. And she did. Medical authorities in Miami ordered an autopsy which confirmed the truth. She died of acute intoxication.

The case made national news only because the victim never touched alcoholic beverages. The late lady was hooked on *just plain water!* By drinking up to four gallons of water a day, she pushed her body too far. The official cause of death was intoxication by water.

That sounds different, but it is a repeat of the same old pattern. Food ceases to nourish and medicine loses its curative properties in massive amounts. Too much is definitely worse than not enough in those categories.

What about work? Many of us derive some of life's greatest pleasure from our chosen careers, especially if we follow God's leadership in full-time Christian service. But work, no matter how wonderful and satisfying, can never substitute for personal devotion unto God. Neither can good works justify neglect of family or punishment of your personal temple of God. The physical body requires a healthy balance between labor and leisure.

Recognizing these dangers, some try too hard to make up for lost time by crash diets or excessive exercise. The opposite extreme, rather than helping, then turns to harm by compounding the original danger. An unconditioned jogger or weekend tennis player invites a fatal heart attack by his sudden urge to treat his body better.

Extremism is a danger even to society. Sociologists observe that no nation or culture has long endured without a stable middle class. Too many poor and too few wealthy invites jealousy, hate, and revolution.

Personal wealth is another extreme some cannot handle. People who come into sudden wealth encounter a new set of problems they are ill-equipped to solve. Tax and investment questions are the easy ones. "Who are my real friends?" "What am I to do now that I no longer need to work?" "Why is everyone after my money?"

Agur, the compiler of Proverbs 30, recognized the dangers of extreme wealth or poverty. "Give me neither poverty nor riches; feed me with the food that is needful for me, lest I be full, and deny thee, and say, 'Who is the Lord?' or lest I be poor, and steal, and profane the name of my God" (vv. 8-9).

Moderation is the key. Seek the middle ground. Paul had it right when he counseled the Philippians, "Let your moderation be known unto all men" (Phil. 4:5, KJV).

Value

Do you sometimes feel worthless or without high commercial value? You realize God views all His children as precious, but right now you wish others would recognize your value as a pastor, parent, teacher, or employee. How difficult to reach your potential when you go unnoticed or unappreciated.

Take heart! You may be like the substance similar to sand which was once used by ancient craftsmen in the production of common glass. Our modern technology produces glass from ordinary sand, so we seldom gave this unusual element a second thought. As late as 1945, one dictionary defined it as "a white, heavy, metallic substance having no apparent value."

Yet in the same year that substance known as uranium powered us into the atomic age. Uranium turned out to be our most valued mineral, worth far more than gold or silver. The uranium boom had finally arrived! Many prospectors searching the vast Western wastelands of America got lucky and became instant millionaires.

Funny thing about uranium, however. It had never changed during those long centuries while people judged it of no apparent value. The difference came in our evaluation of the mineral. We learned that it did have usefulness and thus value. But uranium had remained the same all along.

Like uranium, you and I have inherent and even hidden value. God made us all in His image and for His own purposes. How wonderful and inspiring if people could only see through God's eyes the true value of everyone else. But more important for now is that we individually understand first our own worth before God.

Had Moses listened to the multitudes, he would have given up. To hear them complain at every turn and murmur against him so often must have been a soul-testing experience. His own people condemned him for making that dramatic appearance before the Pharaoh demanding, "Let my people go!"

Earlier they had believed in Moses and rejoiced in his return, but Pharaoh's harsh reprisal changed everything. With backs bent under increased labor of finding straw to make the same number of bricks, they blamed Moses. "It's all your fault, Moses!" That is what they meant by saying, "The Lord look upon you and judge, because you have made us offensive in the sight of Pharaoh" (Ex. 5:21).

But did their wrong opinion of Moses change his true value? No, indeed. Moses was still a chosen vessel of God even if his own people turned against Moses. Centuries later the same people rejected Jesus. "He came to his own home, and his own people received him not" (John 1:11). Jesus proved His love for us and our value to Him by dying in our place. He pointed to the common sparrows, traditionally considered the least important and cheapest of all life.

> Are not two sparrows sold for a penny? And not one of them will fall to the ground without your Father's will. But even the hairs of your head are all numbered. Fear not, therefore; you are of more value than many sparrows (Matt. 10:29-31).

If sparrows and uranium have value, certainly we do also. Be encouraged in God's love for you.

Follow-up

So you make mistakes. Who doesn't? Failure is not the fatal problem. Watch your critical follow up. That is what counts.

When most people fail, they are finished. They quit. But not Robert Fulton. The inventor believed he could build a boat powered by steam rather than sail.

"Fulton's Folly," the crowd called it. Hadn't his earlier boat sunk in France? Now he wanted to repeat the folly in America! A fellow once burned ought to be twice shy.

Fire was a big problem with steam boilers which required lots of fire. But fuel was an even bigger problem. Crowded cargo ships simply had no room for coal or firewood.

The obstacles were many. Every previous attempt had met defeat, but here was a positive thinker who would not quit. Fulton ignored critics and doomsday doubters. He had learned valuable lessons from each failure. All he needed now was money for construction of a new craft.

Now *that* was a problem! Bankers and financiers feared the association with such folly. Only when Fulton promised to keep their names secret did they lend the necessary funds.

Despite all his critics, history testifies that Fulton laughed last. In 1807 his *Clermont* became the world's first successful steamship! It was the beginning of a new era!

Fulton had found the best way to follow up on failure. He learned from his mistakes. Indeed, any bad loss can teach a good lesson.

We can profit from our pitfalls.

"We know that in everything God works for good with those

who love him, who are called according to his purpose" (Rom. 8:28).

Good News

Years ago a California peddler built a lunch wagon on the frame of his three-wheel bicycle. Then he pedaled all over town in search of customers. One day while crossing the railroad tracks beside a factory, he dreamed of selling lots of sandwiches and coffee. He had loaded his wagon heavily in his optimism for a good day.

Trouble came instead. The main axle on his bike wagon broke, stranding his rig on the tracks. Before he could unload enough supplies to pull a lighter wagon to safety, the train appeared. It was too late.

That poor man witnessed the destruction of his dream wagon. And what a wreck it was. Everything was gone except his coffee maker and a few supplies.

A crowd gathered to examine the crash site. The disappointed man could have sat down and cried, but he didn't. He realized that a crowd meant potential customers, so he grabbed a bucket and ran into the factory for hot water. Within minutes he was selling fresh coffee to the curious. Business was booming!

That winning attitude impressed everyone. Soon he was well known as a happy man who made good coffee in bad times. Triumph from tragedy! What he had lost became the beginning of something better! But only when he saw some good in a bad situation.

Sooner or later we all get knocked down. That hurts. How much easier to just give up and stay down. Less pain that way.

But there is no victory in that valley. So look up. Get up. Climb up with God's help. Be a Joseph rising above brotherly betrayal.

Be a Job unwilling to curse God and die in misery because faith would never surrender.

You can be certain God has something better for you than today's defeat in a bad-news world.

"And I am sure that he who began a good work in you will bring it to completion at the day of Jesus Christ" (Phil. 1:6).

Wacky Ways

Have you noticed? When people of prominence behave strangely, they are tolerated as "eccentric." But for the same silly deeds, you and I would be called "crazy."

Cornelius Vanderbilt believed enough in education and religion to bestow several fortunes upon institutions of higher learning. Vanderbilt University and its Divinity School are named for the generous visionary. Yet this same man made sure that each leg of his bed at home rested in a bowl of salt. Why? To scare away evil spirits!

Arthur Wellesley, better known as the Duke of Wellington and victor over Napoleon at Waterloo in 1815, later served as prime minister of England. He was a true gentleman who prided himself on never being late for an appointment. Just to be certain of the exact time, the busy hero regularly consulted six different watches which he carried on his person at all times!

Catherine the Great, empress of Russia in czarist days, wore a wig. Only her hairdresser knew. To keep their secret safe, she confined him to an iron cage in her own bedroom for three years!

George Clemenceau abhorred pajamas and was not one to be caught in his underwear. The World-War-I French statesman slept most nights fully clothed, including shoes and gloves.

How thin is that line between genius and insanity! But why

worry about what people think? These famous folks never seemed so insecure that they tried to protect their personal reputations. Perhaps the rest of us should take note. What people think of us is not nearly as important as we suppose. A healthy measure of self-confidence allows us to be ourselves. If that means a few wacky ways which raises some eyebrows, so what? We don't have to please everyone.

Yet there is One whom we ought to please. God allows us freedom to respond to Him in our own ways because, after all, he created us that way. Each person is unique and different. "So we, though many, are one body in Christ, and individually members one of another. Having gifts that differ according to the grace given to us, let us use them" (Rom. 12:5-6).

Submission

It was a perfect day for the beach, and Carl's friends were with him to enjoy the experience. Best of all, Carl thought, was the opportunity to display his swimming skills. Among the youth in his group, no one could compete with him in the water. There was no doubt in his mind. Carl considered himself an olympic star of the future.

That reckless confidence led Carl to swim far out into the sea. Only a sissy would stay close to shore. What a wonderful time until he realized how tired his body felt. Then fun turned to fear. Could he stay afloat long enough to reach the safety of shore? His muscles strained and failed.

An alert lifeguard recognized danger out in the deep. He had been monitoring the situation and soon plunged into the water. He swam all the way out to the drowning youth and tried to help. Carl was so frightened by that time that he resisted the efforts of his rescuer. Both the lifeguard and the foolish swimmer were nearly drowned in a deadly embrace amid thrashing water.

How can you rescue someone who refuses your help? The lifeguard did the only thing possible. He swam just a few feet away and waited until the drowning lad had exhausted all his strength. Then, just as Carl was about to go under for the last time, the rescuer swiftly moved in.

Carl was by then too weak to resist. He meekly yielded to the superior strength of the lifeguard who pulled his limp body back to the beach.

Therein lies a parable of our human dilemma. We go as far as we can on our own strength before discovering, sooner or later, that our best is not good enough.

We thrash around in life panic-stricken, resisting God's help. God patiently waits for us to waste our strength and admit defeat. Yet some people never will give up to God. Like a wounded animal caught in a corner, they turn against their Creator and Rescuer.

A better course is admitting our failure and accepting the loving embrace of an all-powerful Savior. Submission is the key!

"Submit yourselves therefore to God. Resist the devil and he will flee from you. Draw near to God, and he will draw near to you" (Jas. 4:7-8).

A Shocking Experience

A Communist judge in Yugoslavia had a shocking experience. One should never reach for a light switch while standing in the bathtub.

A jolt of electricity threw him out of the tub and onto the floor. His wife called the doctor who pronounced him dead at the scene.

That was about bedtime, but news like that spreads fast even at night.

They carried the accident victim to a cemetery chapel. Early the next day his body could be properly dressed for a funeral. Before morning, however, the man regained consciousness and found himself in an open casket located in a holding vault beneath the cemetery chapel.

He climbed out of the casket and shook the locked door of the vault. "Help!" The night guard was totally terrified. He wasn't about to hang around and protect the premises any longer.

Later the guard returned with reinforcements. They finally agreed to open the door and release the "corpse" who was complaining so loudly. Yet the judge still wasn't home free. When he phoned his wife in the middle of the night, she took his good news very normally. She fainted, leaving him holding the telephone.

Barefoot and clad only in a white robe, a frustrated judge took to the streets. He desperately sought someone who would accept him back into the land of the living. What a night for the entire community! When he knocked at the doors of friends or neighbors, they shrieked and slammed doors in his face.

At last, he found a friend unaware of his recent "death" and thus had nothing to be explained away. O happy day that dawned! His friend calmly went door to door explaining the good news to family and friends. They were finally prepared to welcome a survivor back to life.

How wonderful it is when people are proven wrong about death. When we believers in Jesus breathe no longer, the worldly wise will pronounce us dead, too.

Ah, but not for long! It may come as a shock to some, but we are going to live again. And that by the testimony of someone who Himself rose from the grave after three days—Jesus Christ.

"I am the resurrection and the life; he who believes in me, though he die, yet shall he live" (John 11:25).

Out of This World

Are you ready? A new company in Houston, Texas, wants to use the latest in space technology to send you into orbit. Literally. It is a final journey that really is out of this world.

Certain restrictions apply for this one-way trip. No luggage, no hurry in departure, and no extended payment plan. They are banking on your cash in advance.

They further promise that no customer will ever worry about mundane matters of comfort. The corpse never complains!

By now you realize this offer concerns the disposal of your final remains. The Texas company offers a dramatic alternative to ordinary burial in the ground.

No longer can people say, "You only go around once in this world." Now you can be guaranteed to go around forever in the Van Allen radiation belt nineteen-hundred miles above the earth.

Forever? Well, the fine print says forever or at least sixty-three million years—whichever comes first.

As an added benefit the company will launch your satellite into a visible orbit. That way your friends on earth can look up and wave as you pass over them! Ten thousand of you sharing the same satellite in one-half ounce containers ought to cause quite a stir below.

How much? The present price tag for this service is thirty-nine-hundred dollars. Cremation is required and costs extra. Don't forget to include shipping fees.

Are they serious? We wonder at such foolishness!

We Christians can count on a better offer from our Creator. We look forward to the Lord's return when the dead in Christ will rise first; then we who are alive, who are left, shall be caught up together with them in the clouds to meet the Lord in the air; and so we shall always be with the Lord (1 Thess. 4:16-17).

Renewal

Ponce de Leon was doomed from the beginning in his search for the elusive secret of eternal youth. Instead of the fountain of youth, he found the frustrations of old age. He should have known better.

Across the vast horizons of human existence, the long shadow of eternity has always outlasted the swiftest of young sprinters or the strongest of old survivors. Time and chance are against us. Solomon long ago observed the futility of flesh because "the race is not to the swift, nor the battle to the strong" (Eccl. 9:11).

We begin life with time as our ally. With each passing year we grow stronger. But, all too soon, time becomes a mortal enemy. Gray hair, wrinkled skin, weak eyes, diminished strength—these are the telltale marks which we must bear as testimony to the relentless march of time tramping over and past our bodies.

But enough of this pessimism! We Christians have better thoughts about our future. With each passing day we move closer to that grand climax of life. We look beyond death to the second coming of our Lord. Jesus is coming again.

Today we are closer to heaven than yesterday. History moves with a sense of purpose because God is in charge. Of what use is a frail, physical body in heaven?

The apostle Paul freely admitted that his body was becoming a burden to him. He compared it to an earthly tent slowly being destroyed with age. He much preferred the heavenly dwelling, the new body in his future.

"So we do not lose heart. Though our outer nature is wasting away, our inner nature is being renewed every day." (2 Cor. 4:16)

That is the secret of growing old gracefully. Let God renew you from within. Then look ahead. What a fabulous future you can have with God!

Pobody's Nerfect!

So you are not perfect. But no one else is either. Not even the editors of the *Encyclopedia Britannica,* that monument to British publishing prestige. Those good people pride themselves on high standards of publishing perfection. Yet an expert seeking errors in a recent edition of their encyclopedia picked at random found over six-hundred glaring examples of outdated or discredited facts.

Some say the perfect book will never be produced on this earth. It has been tried many times without success because, one way or another, errors inevitably appear.

Years ago the esteemed University Press in Glasgow, Scotland, chose to reprint a certain classical work in their attempt at this elusive goal of perfection. They employed six professional proofreaders to check every word of every page. Then they checked again and again. The professionals were satisfied.

Next they turned to amateurs. Galley proofs of each page were displayed in a university hall for two weeks. A handsome reward was offered to anyone who could find any errors. Only after the reward went begging were the publishers convinced they had the perfect book. Every previous error had been corrected for certain.

Well, almost every error. The first day the book rolled off the printing presses, someone found a mistake on the first line of the first page!

Mistakes. Errors. Misjudgments. Let's hear it for erasers and correction fluid!

But more, let's thank our Creator for being the God of a second chance. He does not demand perfection here on earth. He forgives our sins when we humbly repent and confess. He repairs and restores broken relationships between Creator and created.

"If we confess our sins, he is faithful and just, and will forgive our sins and cleanse us from all unrighteousness" (1 John 1:9).

Together

As the song says, some things like love and marriage or a horse and carriage just naturally go together. So do the names of Gilbert and Sullivan, the most productive partnership in musical history. They began when William Gilbert penned clever dialogue with poems and songs. Arthur Sullivan then collaborated as composer who set the script to catchy tunes and orchestral arrangements.

In the quarter century before 1900, this famous pair created fourteen of the world's most popular musicals. They both received the ultimate English honor of knighthood.

Sir William and Sir Arthur made quite a team—except for one problem. They couldn't get along. They kept a constant argument going because Gilbert's sharp wit and cynicism irritated Sullivan's sensitive soul. The personalities of the wordly writer and the moody musician conflicted in the worse way.

Yet the public demanded their continued association. Those contrasting talents somehow complemented each other in a delightful manner. Clearly, they were destined to work together for the enjoyment of all.

So how did Gilbert and Sullivan solve this awkward problem? They resolved to work by correspondence! Postmen acted as intermediaries, delivering their work to a publisher who combined their separate labors into musical masterpieces.

A common cause or a mutual purpose can do much to bring us together. When our lower nature causes separation, look to something higher. Sharing a great dream or serving in an important movement helps us overlook our differences.

Two neighboring families had feuded for some time. Even their children were involved in pretty disputes and arguments. Then a community crisis brought them together one dry day when fire swept down the mountainside toward their homes. For hours every member of both families cooperated in a valiant attempt to beat back the flames. Children brought buckets of water and wet rags to the parents who could then douse smoldering shingles. Parents moved from house to house as the wind shifted and changed the direction of attack.

In the urgency of that hour, they realized just how intertwined were their fates. Both houses would survive, or both would burn. Either way, they would be together. But the drama ended happily with both homes saved and both families united in a memory which overlooked differences of opinion.

Together! What a wonderful idea, a beautiful thought. But the best place to see this in action is the local church where believers in Jesus gather. The eleven-o'clock worship hour may be the last place in North America where people of such wide backgrounds can come together. The differences of race, color, occupation, age, sex, or social standing fade in the presence of Jesus.

"Behold, how good and pleasant it is for brethren to dwell together in unity!" (Ps. 133:1, KJV).

Hope

Alexander the Great was not always called *great.* He could have lived a life of ease in the shadow of his famous father, King Philip of Macedon, who led Greek armies to many victories. Don't strong fathers often beget weak sons?

But Philip's son would never be considered weak. Alexander wept in frustration after conquering most of the known world, that there were no more lands to conquer. Here was a son unwilling to follow in his father's footsteps. He wanted to surpass his father and make a name for himself.

Trained in the best military tradition, Alexander prepared to leave home for foreign fields of battle. He would lead his own armies and conquer his own lands.

But before he left, Alexander did something strange. He divided all his possessions among his friends. Everything he had was theirs to keep whether he came back or not. His friends resisted saying, "But you have kept nothing for yourself." Alexander smiled and disagreed.

"Oh, yes I have. I have kept my hopes. They shall sustain me." And they did.

Hope is often the key to endurance. Life depends upon this positive, practical power. Sensitive doctors have learned to encourage hope among the terminally ill. To bluntly deny any possibility of recovery demoralizes the patient. He will soon give up and die because "Hope deferred maketh the heart sick" (Prov. 13:12, KJV).

Hold on to hope! Prepare for the worst but continue thinking the best. Hope in all things!

"Never flag in zeal, be aglow with the Spirit, serve the Lord. Rejoice in your hope, be patient in tribulation, be constant in prayer" (Rom. 12:11-12).

A thought-provoking painting by the artist Watts depicts an older woman seated on a large globe which is earth. She has obviously suffered much as suggested by dark colors and shadows which dance in the background. Her bandaged eyes suggest despair and discouragement of one who cannot see the way.

In her lap the lady holds a harp with broken strings. They represent her shattered dreams. Only one string remains in service, but this golden string represents hope.

After the viewer's attention focuses upon that string called hope, the mood of the painting seems to change. It is no longer depressing. One can sense in that scene a deep, abiding strength. The silent sufferer holds on in hope.

People today say the world is getting worse. Based only on the evidence of the daily news, we tend to agree. The world brims with murder, robbery, rape, wars, and rumors of war. There is no peace on our planet.

But the Bible promises something better. There's a bright new world coming because God is in charge. We can hold on in hope which in God's Word is presented as the middle virtue between faith and love.

But like all virtues, hope needs a foundation, a reason. Otherwise, we are just whistling in the dark. But there is no darkness with Jesus. Paul identified hope with Jesus Christ. The living Lord indwells and inspires from within the redeemed heart.

"Christ in you, the hope of glory" (Col. 1:27). That's the foundation, the formula for hope guaranteed.

Surrender

Admiral Horatio Nelson, the English hero who twice defeated Napoleon's navy, lived by a civilized code of conduct. As a victor he treated his vanquished enemies with both kindness and courtesy. A defeated opponent was once brought aboard Nelson's flagship for formal ceremonies of surrender. Crossing Nelson's quarterdeck, he briskly approached his conqueror and offered an outstretched hand.

It was an obvious attempt to trade upon Nelson's gentle spirit in making a grand pretension that the two remained equals. The great English admiral refused that role. With his own hand remaining at his side, Nelson firmly decreed: "Your sword first—and then your hand."

Some people presume to meet their Maker in just as casual an encounter. If the time must come when they stand before Him, they somehow expect to bluff their way past a gentle, gracious God.

Not so! When the unredeemed are summoned before God for final judgment, they will approach His throne with empty hands and bowed heads. They shall stand silently in total defeat before a divine Presence absolutely awesome in majesty. No excuses. No pretense. The sword must be surrendered in complete submission. God is not an equal but the Creator and sovereign Judge of all the universe.

Better to submit willingly now in life before death. An independent, rebellious attitude brings eternal death. But we can trust God to deal graciously toward a saved sinner with a surrendered spirit.

John advised believers to live now for Jesus and look forward to that final moment when Jesus returns to close out this age. "And now, little children, abide in him, so that when he appears we may have confidence and not shrink from him in shame at his coming" (1 John 2:28).

The basis of this confidence is not our good deeds or discovered rewards but the nature of God.

> So we know and believe the love God has for us. God is love, and he who abides in love abides in God, and God abides in him. And this is love perfected with us, that we may have confidence for the day of judgment (1 John 4:16-17).

Duty

Military historians generally concede to Britain the honor of the greatest naval tradition among seafaring nations. And who is the greatest among their heroes? Admiral Horatio Nelson.

Every American schoolboy remembers that the Duke of Wellington defeated Napoleon's army in Europe at Waterloo once. But the English remember how Nelson decisively defeated Napoleon's navy twice!

In the 1798 Battle of the Nile, Nelson destroyed the French fleet and cut off Napoleon's army which had conquered Egypt. The little general had to desert his beleaguered army and sneak back to France in humiliation.

Napoleon later regrouped with a Spanish alliance and again threatened Europe. With only twenty-seven assorted vessels under his command, Nelson met a vastly superior force of thirty-three warships. Before the battle Nelson hoisted his now famous signal. "England expects every man will do his duty."

Then developed one of the world's most memorable naval encounters in which the English admiral directed his smaller fleet to a brilliant attack in close quarters. It was a startling success.

A sharpshooter delivered the only blow of consequence from the French fleet. Nelson, the one-eyed, one-armed fighter who had been wounded many times before, fell mortally wounded. In his last moments, he learned that all thirty-three opposing warships were destroyed. The dying Nelson declared, "Thank God, I have done my duty."

Duty. Men willingly die in performing their duty to country. Nations grow great when citizens rise to the occasions of duty. But sometimes people dismiss duty and make demands instead. They expect more than freedom. Let others feed them also!

People treat God the same way. They want a one-way, delivery service of divine blessings. As if God existed only to make us happy by responding to our every wish and whim.

But God is not our servant. It is we who are servants unto the King of kings. Ours is a duty to serve the divine.

Are you performing your proper duty unto God? Can you say, "Thank God, I have done my duty"?

"So you also, when you have done all that is commanded you, say, 'We are unworthy servants; we have only done what was our duty'" (Luke 17:10).

Index of Scripture Texts

Genesis
- 1:1 ... 82
- 2:25 ... 31
- 3:7 ... 31
- 19:13 ... 51

Exodus
- 5:21 ... 118

Judges
- 16:30 ... 44

1 Kings
- 3:5 ... 108
- 3:9 ... 108
- 3:11-12 ... 108
- 15:12, 14 ... 65

2 Kings
- 7:9 ... 28, 73
- 21:3 ... 65

2 Chronicles
- 16:9 ... 93

Psalms
- 24:3 ... 64
- 33:18 ... 93
- 34:15 ... 93
- 56:3 ... 59

　　　　　69:7 25
　　　　　90:12 108
　　　　　91:11-12 52
　　　　　94:9 93
　　　　　100:3 82
　　　　　107:26-27 67
　　　　　111:10 109
　　　　　118:24 56
　　　　　121:1 54
　　　　　130:1 67
　　　　　133:1 129
　　　　　148:1 64
Proverbs
　　　　　13:12 130
　　　　　21:2 87
　　　　　23:7 37
　　　　　30:8-9 117
Ecclesiastes
　　　　　1:9 100
　　　　　3:1 56
　　　　　9:11 126
Isaiah
　　　　　12:2 59
　　　　　14:13-14 64
Matthew
　　　　　4:4 71
　　　　　4:8-9 65
　　　　　5:1-11 57
　　　　　5:11-12 26
　　　　　6:11 56
　　　　　6:34 58
　　　　　10:29-31 118
　　　　　16:16-17, 23 113
　　　　　16:27 91

Index of Scripture Texts

18:10 52
20:13-15 75
22:30 51
24:3-7 28
24:21, 29 18
25:41, 46 91
25:31-32 90
25:41 52
26:31, 33, 35 113
26:52 36
27:47 14
28:6 42
28:20 34

Mark
3:16 113
8:38 51

Luke
6:38 103
12:8 91
12:9 91
12:2-3 32
12:4 39
15:10 51
17:10 134
23:46 44

John
1:11 118
1:51 51
5:22-23 91
5:24 50
6:33, 35 71
9:1-5 80
10:29 39
11:25 124

Acts

16:33 .... 19, 20
20:25 49
1:8 61
7:60 44
14:22 19
15:39 110
26:26 48

Romans

2:6 91
5:3-5 .... 19, 84
8:18 .... 59, 60
8:28 .... 19, 89, 120
8:31-32 12
8:32 97
8:33-34 13
8:35 14
8:37 57
8:38 .... 51, 52, 62
8:39 69
12:5-6 122
12:11-12 131
14:12 91

1 Corinthians

4:5 75
6:3 51
10:13 104
13:4-5 88
15:58 83

2 Corinthians

2:14 95
4:16 127
4:16 30
5:10 91

5:17	98, 100
6:2	56
9:6	103
11:14	63
11:23	34
11:26	35
12:9	23
12:10	23

Galatians

6:9	83, 102

Ephesians

2:2	64
2:10	82
1:20-21	66
3:18-19	15
4:9	68
6:12	54, 64

Philippians

1:6	111, 112
1:12-14	80
2:3-4	88
3:13-14	57, 114
4:5	117
4:13	105
4:19	78, 105

Colossians

1:27	131
2:10	54
2:15	54

1 Thessalonians

4:16-17	126
4:16-18	68

1 Timothy

5:21	51

2 Timothy
- 1:12 ... 34
- 4:11 ... 111

Hebrews
- 1:14 ... 51
- 4:13 ... 32
- 13:8 ... 98

James
- 2:17, 26 ... 86
- 4:7 ... 52
- 4:7-8 ... 123
- 5:14-15 ... 77

1 Peter
- 2:12 ... 86

1 John
- 1:9 ... 128
- 2:1-2 ... 91
- 2:28 ... 133
- 4:4 ... 52, 63
- 4:16-17 ... 133
- 4:18 ... 53

Jude
- 1:6 ... 52

Revelation
- 2:10 ... 106
- 6 ... 28
- 12:9 ... 52

Index of Names

Adam 31, 93
Adams 61
Agrippa 48
Agur 117
Alexander the Great 130
Arnold, Benedict 73, 74
Asa 64, 93
Augustus III 30
Baal 64
Barnabas 110
Beecher, Henry Ward 111
Bonaparte, Napoleon 112, 121, 132
Carlyle, Thomas 59, 60
Caruso, Enrico 100, 101
Carver, George Washington 76, 77
Catherine the Great 97, 98, 121
Chang 85
Cheatham, Mary 50
Clemenceau, George 121
Cummings, Jr., Marshall George 90
David 74
Degrafinried, Louise 38, 39
de Leon, Ponce 126
Douglas, Stephen F. 109

Duffield, W.W. 82, 83
Edison, Thomas 96, 97, 107, 109, 110
Elijah 64
Ellsworth, Henry 99
Eng 85
Eve 31, 93
Francis of Assisi 46
Franklin, Benjamin 115
Fulton, Robert 119
Gilbert, William 128, 129
Grant, Ulysses S. 112
Hanani 93
Hannibal 105, 106
Herschel, Sir William 60, 61
Hezekiah 65
Hitler 14
Houston, Sam 77, 78
James, Jesse 42
Job 121
John Mark 110, 111
Jones, Stormie 50, 51
Joseph 30, 31, 120
Josiah 65
Judas 113
Jude 52
Keller, Helen 19, 20
Kelley, Grace 53
Kirk, Bob 94
Lardner, Dionysius 80, 81
Lefferts, Marshall 96, 97
LeVerrier 61
Lincoln, Abraham 24, 109
Livingstone, Dr. David 54, 55
Longfellow, Henry Wadsworth 95

Index of Names

Luo, Jay	107
Mallon, Mary	86, 87
Manasseh	65
Moody, Eric	33
Moody, D. L.	59
Moses	118
Nelson, Admiral Horatio	132, 133, 134
Nobel, Alfred	61, 62
O'Bryan, Ronald C.	12
Otis, Elisha	66
Pasteur, Louis	112
Prince Rainier	53
Raleigh, Sir Walter	44, 45
Roosevelt, Theodore	22, 23
Royal, Daryl	59
Samson	22, 44
Samuel	74
Satan	63, 65, 113
Saul	74
Schulz, Charlie	114, 115
Sedor, Walter	70
Simom Peter	113
Silas	110
Solomon	100, 108, 109, 126
Spafford, Horatio	35, 36
Stanley, Henry M.	115
Stephen	12, 44
Stetson, John B.	79
Stevens, Joseph P.	92
Stevenson, Robert Louis	83, 84
Stanley, Henry M.	54, 55, 115
Sullivan Ann	20
Sullivan, Arthur	128, 129
Smith-Taylor, Bishop William	43

Thomas 48, 49
Typhoid Mary.................................87
Vanderbilt, Cornelius........................ 121
Watts 131
Webster, Daniel 102, 103
Wellesley, Arthur 121
Wellington, Duke of 121, 133
Wesley, John 46
Windrow, Sr., Paul...........................38
Zimmerman, Lyman & Thomza 88, 89